ACCENTS ON SHAKESPEARE

General Editor: TERENCE HAWKES

Shakespeare in the Present

Shakespeare in the Present is a stunning collection of essays by Terence Hawkes, which engage with, explain and explore 'presentism'. Presentism is a critical manoeuvre that uses relevant aspects of the contemporary as a crucial trigger for its investigations. It deliberately begins with the material present and lets that set the interrogative agenda. This book suggests ways in which its principles may be applied to aspects of Shakespeare's plays.

Hawkes concentrates on two main areas in which presentism impacts on the study of Shakespeare. The first is the concept of 'devolution' in British politics. The second is presentism's commitment to a reversal of conceptual hierarchies, such as primary/secondary and past/present, and the interaction between performance and reference. The result is to sophisticate and expand our notion of performing and to refocus interest on what the early modern theatre meant by the activity it termed 'playing'.

Terence Hawkes is Emeritus Professor of English at Cardiff University. He is the author of a number of books on literary theory and on Shakespeare, including *Structuralism and Semiotics* (1977), *That Shakespeherian Rag* (1986) and *Meaning by Shakespeare* (1992). He is also General Editor of the *Accents on Shakespeare* series published by Routledge.

ACCENTS ON SHAKESPEARE
General Editor: TERENCE HAWKES

It is more than twenty years since the New Accents series helped to establish 'theory' as a fundamental and continuing feature of the study of literature at the undergraduate level. Since then, the need for short, powerful 'cutting edge' accounts of and comments on new developments has increased sharply. In the case of Shakespeare, books with this sort of focus have not been readily available. **Accents on Shakespeare** aims to supply them.

Accents on Shakespeare volumes will either 'apply' theory, or broaden and adapt it in order to connect with concrete teaching concerns. In the process, they will also reflect and engage with the major developments in Shakespeare studies of the last ten years.

The series will lead as well as follow. In pursuit of this goal it will be a two-tiered series. In addition to affordable, 'adoptable' titles aimed at modular undergraduate courses, it will include a number of research-based books. Spirited and committed, these second-tier volumes advocate radical change rather than stolidly reinforcing the status quo.

Shakespeare in the Present

TERENCE HAWKES

London and New York

First published 2002
by Routledge
11 New Fetter Lane,
London EC4P 4EE

Simultaneously published in
the USA and Canada
by Routledge
29 West 35th Street,
New York, NY 10001

Routledge is an imprint of the
Taylor & Francis Group

© 2002 Terence Hawkes

Typeset in Baskerville by Wearset Ltd,
Boldon, Tyne and Wear
Printed and bound in Great Britain by
TJ International Ltd, Padstow,
Cornwall

British Library Cataloguing in
Publication Data

A catalogue record for this book is
available from the British Library

Library of Congress Cataloging in
Publication Data

A catalog record for this book has been
requested

ISBN 0–415–26195–3 (hbk)
ISBN 0–415–26196–1 (pbk)

To Ann, always

Contents

General editor's preface

In our time, the field of literary studies has rarely been a settled, tranquil place. Indeed, for over two decades, the clash of opposed theories, prejudices and points of view has made it more of a battlefield. Echoing across its most beleaguered terrain, the student's weary complaint 'Why can't I just pick up Shakespeare's plays and read them?' seems to demand a sympathetic response.

Nevertheless, we know that modern spectacles will always impose their own particular characteristics on the vision of those who unthinkingly don them. This must mean, at the very least, that an apparently simple confrontation with, or pious contemplation of, the text of a four-hundred-year-old play can scarcely supply the grounding for an adequate response to its complex demands. For this reason, a transfer of emphasis from 'text' towards 'context' has increasingly been the concern of critics and scholars since the Second World War: a tendency that has perhaps reached its climax in more recent movements such as new historicism or cultural materialism.

A consideration of the conditions – social, political, or economic – within which the play came to exist, from which it derives and to which it speaks will certainly make legitimate demands on the attention of any well-prepared student nowadays. Of course, the serious pursuit of those interests will also inevitably start to undermine ancient and inherited prejudices, such as the supposed distinction between 'foreground' and 'background' in literary studies. And even the slightest awareness of the pressures of gender or of race, or the most cursory glance at the role played by that strange creature 'Shakespeare' in our cultural politics, will reinforce a similar turn towards questions that sometimes appear scandalously 'non-literary'. It seems clear that very different and unsettling notions of the ways in which literature might be addressed can hardly be avoided. The worrying truth is that nobody can just pick up Shakespeare's plays and read them. Perhaps – even more worrying – they never could.

The aim of *Accents on Shakespeare* is to encourage students and teachers to explore the implications of this situation by means of an engagement with the major developments in Shakespeare studies over recent years. It will offer a continuing and challenging reflection on those ideas through a series of multi- and single-author books, which will also supply the basis for adapting or augmenting them in the light of changing concerns.

Accents on Shakespeare also intends to lead as well as follow. In pursuit of this goal, the series will operate on more than one level. In addition to titles aimed at modular undergraduate courses, it will include a number of books embodying polemical, strongly argued cases aimed at expanding the horizons of a specific aspect of the subject and at challenging the preconceptions on which it is based. These volumes will not be learned 'monographs' in any traditional sense. They will, it is hoped, offer a platform for the work of the liveliest younger scholars and teachers at their most outspoken and provocative. Committed and contentious, they will be reporting from the forefront of current critical activity and will have something new to say. The fact that each book in the series promises a Shakespeare inflected in terms of a specific urgency should ensure that, in the present as in the recent past, the accent will be on change.

Terence Hawkes

Acknowledgements

Earlier versions of some of this material have benefited, I hope, from initial airings in a variety of places. These include journals such as *Textual Practice*, *The London Review of Books*, and *Shakespeare Jahrbuch*. I am grateful for the opportunity to refashion, recast and even (most transforming of all stratagems) to repeat it. Various colleagues in Britain and abroad have been kind enough to allow me to address their students on related matters and thus to experience the pleasure and draw on the help that their remarks invariably supply. Christy Desmet, John Drakakis, Balz Engler, Ewan Fernie, Peter Holland, Kiernan Ryan, Robert Sawyer and Stanley Wells have all at various times been convivial hosts as well as valued critics. The comments of Robert Weimann, Catherine Belsey, Richard Levin, David Hawkes and Hugh Grady have also, over the years, proved never less than stimulating. Robert Stradling made his expert historian's advice freely available to me, as did Scott Newton. Charlotte McBride was the most patient of graduate students. All mistakes, misconceptions, confusions and errors of judgement remain, unfortunately, my own. My thanks are also due to Hardy Cook, indefatigable editor of *SHAKSPER: The Global Electronic Shakespeare Conference*, whose website still permits both my electronic effusions and his horde of acute and occasionally irascible contributors their sometimes scathing but always bracing responses to them. My greatest debt, repeated over the years but changing only in its increase, remains to my wife.

1
Introduction

Pulling Ranke

This collection of essays doesn't offer the methodical exposition of a thesis. It's more a series of short-winded responses to aspects of the changing climate in Shakespeare studies. Currently prominent amongst them is one that urges us to read the plays 'historically': to reinsert them into the context in which they first came to be, and on which, it's said, their intelligibility depends. Our aim for Shakespeare should be to 'restore Shakespeare's artistry to the earliest conditions of its realisation...' and to 'restore his works to the specific imaginative and material circumstances in which they were written and engaged'. Only when we do this, can we hope to confront the Bard's 'historical specificity'.[1]

Of course, if the alternative is to deal with plays in blissful ignorance of their historical context, to impose on them, as many teachers unthinkingly seem to do, some kind of absurd contemporaneity with ourselves, usually justified by windy rhetoric about the Bard's 'universality', then perhaps historical specificity of some sort is an acceptable antidote. However, that kind of artlessness doesn't seem to be the main target. One of the biggest obstacles to reading Shakespeare historically, says David Kastan, is 'theory'. Theory's stress on the critic's 'situatedness' in the present results in a self-regarding focus that irrevocably contaminates any contact with the past. Only if we confront the plays' texts in terms, not of the critic's present situation, but of the 'actual conditions of their production and reception', stressing both their 'particularity and contingency', can we defeat the Bard's most sinister enemy. Its name is 'presentism'.[2]

The principal talisman capable of warding off this spectre is called 'facts': facts about specific historical conditions that have determined the reading and writing of literature, facts about the material circumstances of literary production, facts about how books and playscripts were actually produced, sold and received. Retrieved and analysed by the scholar, these facts will lay bare, not the author's unique meaning, concealed within the text, but the extent to which the text itself speaks of 'the corporate activities that have brought it into being'.[3]

All well and good, but – a matter of tone – what does that reiterated 'restore' imply? Does it hint at the recovery of a lost purity, of a final arrival at truth-revealing origins, of the Restoration at last of the genuine monarchy of genius, even of a more fundamental confrontation, no longer in a glass, darkly, but now face to face? It's true that a looming, obtrusive present would certainly blur the outlines of any Grail worth grasping. And if the aim of historical scholarship were simply to establish 'how it really was' – in the words of Leopold von Ranke, *wie es eigentlich gewesen* – then the present can only be an intervening, distracting fog that needs to be pierced or blown away. But the present's relation to the past is surely a subtler matter than that. All restorations face one major problem. Reaching backwards, they can't afford to examine the position in the present from which that manoeuvre is undertaken. As a result, they discount the nature of the choosing and the omission, the selections and suppressions that determine it. Yet to avoid the pitfall by taking one's present situation fully into account seems inevitably to compromise the project. Genuinely to capture, or repeat, the past is of course fundamentally impossible for a variety of other reasons. In fact, the attempt to do so, an issue discussed in Chapter 8, usually risks an engagement, not with sameness, but with the very motive forces that produce difference. Restoration may aim to be the thief of time, but it's a notoriously unsuccessful one.

For none of us can step beyond time. It can't be drained out of our experience. As a result, the critic's own 'situatedness' does not – cannot – contaminate the past. In effect, it constitutes the only means by which it's possible to see the past and perhaps comprehend it. And since we can only see the past through the eyes of the present, few serious historians would deny that the one has a major influence on their account of the other. Of course we should read Shakespeare historically. But given that history results from a never-ending dialogue between past and present, how can we decide whose historical circumstances will have priority in that process, Shakespeare's, or our own?

To reduce history to a series of isolateable, untheorised 'facts', or neutrally analysable 'texts', is in any case unproductive. Facts do not speak for themselves. Nor do texts. This doesn't mean that facts or texts don't exist. It does mean that all of them are capable of genuinely contradictory meanings, none of which has any independent, 'given', undeniable, or self-evident status. Indeed, they don't speak at all unless and until they are inserted into and perceived as part of specific discourses which impose their own shaping requirements and agendas. We choose the facts. We choose the texts. We do the inserting. We do the perceiving. Facts and texts, that is to say, don't simply speak, don't merely mean. *We* speak, *we* mean, *by* them.

Living in the present

It's time to look at presentism again. History is far too important to be left to scholars who believe themselves able to make contact with a past unshaped by their own concerns. All history, said Benedetto Croce, is contemporary history. The present ranks, not as an obstacle to be avoided, nor as a prison to be escaped from. Quite the reverse: it's a factor actively to be sought out, grasped and perhaps, as a result, understood. If an intrusive, shaping awareness of ourselves, alive and active in our own world, defines us, then it deserves our closest attention. Paying the present that degree of respect might more profitably be judged, not as a 'mistake', egregious and insouciant, blandly imposing a tritely modern perspective on whatever texts confront it, but rather as the basis of a critical stance whose engagement with the text is of a particular character. A Shakespeare criticism that takes that on board will not yearn to speak with the dead. It will aim, in the end, to talk to the living.

There are two areas in which presentism seems particularly suited to make a significant contribution to the study of Shakespeare and the following essays attempt to engage with both of them. The first concerns the recent development of 'devolution' in British politics. The commitment to parliaments or assemblies in Wales, Scotland and Northern Ireland made in 1997, and realised in 1999, ranks as one of the major constitutional changes of our present, even though its implications have yet fully to be absorbed in the United Kingdom, or indeed grasped by observers from abroad.[4] The whole process requires that the 'Great Britain' project, chronicled and championed repeatedly in the Shakespearean canon, must henceforth be seen, not just as the opening of a new and apparently permanent world order, but as the beginning of an enterprise that, after four hundred years, has now reached its conclusion.

This cannot help but generate intricate realignments of our responses to a number of Shakespeare's plays, and I have tried to make that point in my analysis of two of them in Chapters 3 and 4. That texts can never be read after 1999 in quite the same way that they could be read before that date, that their 'meaning', now thoroughly suffused with different levels and intensities of irony, seems to change before our eyes, offers a fine example of how the present helps to mould the past. It's something that the zealous pursuit of *wie es eigentlich gewesen* not only cannot supply but must, to some extent, obscure.

The second area of potential interest arises from presentism's crucial investment in the reversal of apparently immutable conceptual hierarchies such as primary/secondary, past/present, discussed in Chapter 2. After all, a fully paid-up presentist will always feel entitled to ask how the influence of Shakespeare on Marx or Freud matches up to the influence of Marx or Freud on Shakespeare. Even Hitler, as Chapter 5 suggests, made an impression on the Bard. Presentism thus finds itself inevitably predisposed to engage sympathetically with those 'inverting' tendencies that have lately begun to undermine some of the inherited priorities governing our perception of Shakespeare's plays. Placing emphasis on the present can't help but connect fruitfully with the current realignment of critical responses that stresses the *performance* of a play as much as its 'reference': that looks at what the play *does*, here and now in the theatre, as well as – or even against – what it *says* in terms of the world to which its written text refers. Presentism thus highlights what has been termed drama's 'performative' function: a feature that always operates concurrently with, and perhaps as a modification of, its referential function. The effect of that realignment is to sophisticate and expand our notion of performing, and to refocus interest on what the early modern theatre meant by the activity it termed 'playing'.

Playing, as distinct from acting, evidently embraced a far broader spectrum of activity, both on the stage and in the audience, than appears to modern eyes. Our systematic academic privileging of a play's text over its performance comes to seem, as a result, oddly prejudiced. Chapters 6 and 7 explore that extended and complex sense of the term 'play', which, in its fifteenth- and sixteenth-century context, included the vast, unsystematised, and often non-verbal range of communicative traffic always evident in the here-and-now immediacy that binds performer to audience.

Earlier versions of a number of these essays have been published separately, as ideas and the occasions that called them forth developed. Their point of view remains, I hope, nevertheless cohesive, and the 'essay' mode, I trust, not entirely inappropriate to the project. If Chapter 2 does to some extent outline a case for a different kind of criticism, the pieces that follow aim, however unsystematically, to justify it. Perhaps, in their diversity, they might even be allowed to mimic as well as probe the disconcerting experience that these days seems an inevitable part of living in the present.

2

The Heimlich Manoeuvre

In custody

We can begin with two eruptions. The first occurs in the middle of Matthew Arnold's famous essay of 1864, 'The Function of Criticism At The Present Time'. Arnold has been addressing the linked questions of the true nature of literary criticism on the one hand and the true nature of British national culture on the other. If the first is ever to engage fruitfully with the second, he argues, literary criticism must become a de-politicised 'absolutely and entirely independent' activity. Only then will it be able to confront and finally defeat what he calls the 'retarding and vulgarizing' accounts of the current national way of life recently put forward by two home-grown journalist/politicians, Sir Charles Adderley and Mr John Arthur Roebuck.

Then, casting round for an example of something concrete to set against the fatuous self-satisfaction of these apologists, with their cant about 'our unrivalled happiness' as members of 'the old Anglo-Saxon race ... the best breed in the whole world', he suddenly quotes – out of the blue – from a newspaper account of a specific criminal case:

> A shocking child murder has just been committed at Nottingham. A girl named Wragg left the workhouse there on Saturday morning with her young illegitimate child. The child was soon afterwards found dead on Mapperley Hills, having been strangled. Wragg is in custody.[1]

The impact of that, even today, is considerable. A nugget of genuine domestic Britishness, the case of Wragg is curiously disturbing at a number of levels. *Nomen est omen.* The 'hideous' name *Wragg*, Arnold comments, itself challenges the pretensions of 'our old Anglo-Saxon breed ... the best in the whole world' by showing 'how much that is harsh and ill-favoured' there is in that best. A literary criticism that 'serves the cause of perfection' by insisting on the contrast between pretension and reality in society must begin precisely here, at home. And although Mr Roebuck may not think much of an adversary who 'replies to his defiant songs of triumph only by murmuring under his breath *Wragg is in custody*', in no other way (says Arnold) will these songs of triumph be induced gradually to moderate themselves.[2] He doesn't consider whether Mr Roebuck (*nomen est omen* indeed) might have been more effectively challenged by the murmuring of what a local newspaper reports to have been Wragg's own piteous, yet oddly piercing, cry at her trial, setting her present state of custody tellingly against its opposite: 'I should never have done it if I had had a home for him'.[3]

Homeboy

Wragg's is a voice – and a name – that could easily have issued, a generation later, from the depths of T.S. Eliot's *The Waste Land.* Like the snatches of conversation about pregnancy and marriage, and the drunken demotic pub-talk of that poem, her words somehow seem to speak from the domestic centre of a culture – indeed they focus on house and 'home' – whilst at the same time signalling a fundamental estrangement from it.

In fact the second eruption occurs in a critical essay of T.S. Eliot's. It is one with a similar purpose to Arnold's, indicated by its employment of the same title: 'The Function of Criticism' (1923). In response partly to the vapourisings of the critic

John Middleton Murry, Eliot here also takes up the question of literary criticism and the nature of genuine Englishness. Murry has argued that the latter is to be found vested in something that he terms the 'inner voice' of the nation: 'The English writer, the English divine, the English statesman, inherit no rules from their forebears; they inherit only this: a sense that in the last resort they must depend on the inner voice'.[4] Eliot's sensitivity to the imperatives of tradition, and his carefully honed New England sensibility (perhaps additionally burnished, as befits a recent immigrant, with newly Englished zeal), of course included a positive commitment to an inheritance from forebears. As a result, he immediately recoils from this 'inner voice' of Old England. Admitting, coldly, that the statement appears 'to cover certain cases', he begins a withering attack:

> The inner voice, in fact, sounds remarkably like an old principle which has been formulated by an elder critic in the now familiar phrase of 'doing as one likes'.

– and then the ice cracks and a most startling and memorable image suddenly erupts:

> The possessors of the inner voice ride ten in a compartment to a football match at Swansea, listening to the inner voice, which breathes the eternal message of vanity, fear, and lust.[5]

Moral revelations vouchsafed in the corridor of a train of the Great Western Railway (as it then was), whilst pulling out of Paddington Station from London *en route* to Swansea, are no doubt few and far between. But even if they lack the force of holy writ, their impact can apparently be considerable. Faced with what might be called an excluding plenitude of rowdy Englishness, Eliot's criticism here starts to draw on rhythmic and metaphorical skills developed in the cause of the modernist aesthetic. What suddenly surfaces is nothing less than the nucleus of a kind of *imagist* poem, something that Ezra Pound characterised as 'an intellectual and emotional complex in an instant of time'. Characteristically – like Pound's own famous 'In a station of the Metro'

The apparition of these faces in the crowd;
Petals on a wet, black bough.

– it involves modern urban transport systems, with their enclosed spaces and vivid, if ephemeral, visual contacts. Ultimately, it offers an image both fleeting and concrete, confirming – as Richard Aldington put it – that an imagist poem properly manifests a 'hardness, as of cut stone'.[6] Yet it is also clear and concise, mimicking the episodic glance of the male urban *flâneur*. It meets, almost precisely, the requirement of T.E. Hulme for a 'visual, concrete language', which '... always endeavours to *arrest* you and to make you continuously see a physical thing' (*Speculations*).[7] And when the undoubtedly arrested Eliot inspected that intensely physical railway compartment, what he saw was a militant Englishness – roused, perhaps by the prospect of foreign parts, i.e. Swansea – which in a suddenly disturbing, not to say nationalist, mode seemed to have no resting place, no room, no home to offer him.

Easily Freudened

The concept of 'home' in that expanded sense is perhaps crucially developed for the twentieth century in Freud's well-known paper of 1919, *Das Unheimliche*.[8] Its argument aims to distinguish a particular class of, or core of feeling within, the general field of 'the frightening', which could justify the use of a special name. Freud's immediate target is the apparently stable opposition between the *heimlich*, the 'intimate' or 'domestic', and the *unheimlich*, the strange or 'uncanny'.[9] His central tactic is to unpick and ultimately to dissolve that opposition.

Freud's case is that the 'uncanny' is not simply the new and the unfamiliar. Something has to be added to it in order to give it its 'uncanny' quality, and that something is, disturbingly, already well known to us: 'the uncanny (*unheimlich*) is that class of the frightening which leads back to what is known of old and long familiar'.[10] More disturbingly, 'the *unheimlich* is what was once *heimisch*, familiar; the prefix 'un' is the token of repression'. Thus the uncanny, says Freud, invariably involves something 'which ought to have remained hidden, but has come to light'.[11]

One key to the mystery lies in what the paper terms 'an examination of linguistic usage'.[12] This reveals that the apparent polarities *heimlich/unheimlich* are not truly opposed. The 'familiar' begins to reveal surprising links with the 'not known'. Indeed, as the different shades of meaning derived from *heimlich* develop, Freud argues, they start to exhibit qualities identical with their opposites until, on the one hand, the word 'means what is familiar and agreeable, and on the other, what is concealed and kept out of sight'.[13] This migration of meaning finally reveals, as he puts it in a classic deconstructive manoeuvre, the interdependence of the terms: 'Thus *heimlich* is a word the meaning of which develops in the direction of ambivalence, until it finally coincides with its opposite *unheimlich*. *Unheimlich* is in some way or other a sub-species of *heimlich*.'[14]

It is obviously tempting to try to situate Matthew Arnold's notion of a *heimlich* English culture in this context. His essay not only considers Englishness in terms of what Edward Said calls 'an aggressive sense of nation, home, community and belonging', of being 'at home' or 'in place' in a particular sphere.[15] He defines it at last and most powerfully by pointing to the boundary beyond which the 'placeless' or the 'homeless' or the 'uncanny' begins. This is exactly where we encounter Wragg. She erupts in Arnold's text as a horrific, homeless spectre, revealing a suppressed dimension of the culture that a properly directed criticism will force us to confront. Such a criticism's last, and best, function, Arnold seems to be saying, is to tell us what our 'home' culture is really like, and it does that by enabling us to see Wragg clearly, as a powerful signifier whose reiteration is enough to puncture the pomposities of Messrs Adderley and Roebuck. Criticism's very detachment from the political, practical and polemical enables it, says Arnold, to confront these gentlemen with what their vision occludes: it points to an *unheimlich* suppressed by, but unavoidably included within, the English *heimlich*. Once more the focus is on nomenclature:

> *Wragg!* If we are to talk of ideal perfection, of 'the best in the whole world', has any one reflected what a touch of grossness in our race, what an original shortcoming in the more delicate spiritual perceptions, is shown by the natural

growth amongst us of such hideous names – Higginbottom,
Stiggins, Bugg! In Ionia and Attica they were luckier in this
respect than 'the best race in the world': by the Ilissus
there was no Wragg, poor thing![16]

Recognition of the wretched Wragg and her plight is not only
seen as the central concern and duty of responsible criticism,
but, in the course of Arnold's analysis, it becomes clear that her
homelessness, like the plight of the homeless everywhere,
serves to define what we mean by 'home'. Wragg thus acts as a
boundary marker, a gibbet and a dangling body that proclaims
the limit of civilisation as we know it, the absolute distinctions
of an 'English' discourse, the end of the real, the natural, the
'inside', the 'superior' and the domestic, and the beginning of
the strange, the unnatural, the 'outside', the 'inferior' and the
uncanny. Wragg, in short, marks the spot where the *heimlich* is
defined by the fact that the *unheimlich* appears.

The spectre continually haunting the notion of 'criticism', as
described by Arnold and many others since, is that of its apparently essential subsequence: its status as something merely
repetitive, something that is always *ex post facto*, already preceded. Michel Foucault's disingenuous statement that the hierarchical relationship primary/secondary, text/commentary is
permanent, regardless of the nature of the documents that take
on these functions, offers a classic formulation. He grants that
'This differentiation is certainly neither stable, nor constant,
nor absolute. There is not, on the one side, the category of fundamental or creative discourses, given for all time, and on the
other, the mass of discourses which repeat, gloss, and
comment'.[17] None the less he claims that the principle of a
differentiation will continuously be 'put back into play'. We can
annul one or other of the terms of the relation, but we cannot
'do away with the relation itself'.

Foucault goes on to argue that 'in what is broadly called
commentary', the hierarchy that pertains between primary and
secondary texts plays two complementary roles. The 'dominance of the primary text, its permanence, its status as a discourse which can always be re-actualised' seems to make for an
'open possibility of speaking'. On the other hand, the 'only
role' open to commentary is to repeat: 'to say at last what was
silently articulated "beyond", in the text.' Caught in a paradox,

the commentary must 'say for the first time what had, nonethe-
less, already been said, and must tirelessly repeat what had,
however, never been said'. It offers a 'repetition in disguise', at
whose furthest reach there lurks the spectre of 'mere recitation'.

The first casualty of any probing of the notion of an unchal-
lengeable relationship between primary and secondary will of
course be that idea of repetition. Repetition presupposes a
primary to which it is itself inevitably secondary. However,
Freud's notion of the *unheimlich* immediately brings that relationship into question. Repetition of the same thing, he argues,
is a major source of the uncanny, and it can finally be defined in
terms that stress exactly that: it is that class of frightening things
'in which the frightening element can be shown to be something repressed which *recurs*'.[18] Freud's larger theory of repetition is of course fully developed in *Beyond The Pleasure Principle*,
on which he was working concurrently with his revision of *Das
Unheimliche*. There, as part of a fundamental 'need to restore an
earlier state of things', repetition achieves a kind of primary initiating status as it comes to be linked to the death drive.[19] And
certainly when *heimlich* and *unheimlich* merge, the Foucauldian
'secondary' seems to mingle with and almost to usurp its
'primary'. Here, at least, the so-called 'relation itself' between
them starts to seem collusive, rather than 'given', and the persistent sense that the one lies at the heart of the other hints at a
potential obliteration of the distinction between the two.

For Arnold, it is clear that literary criticism is the activity
that, drawing the uncanny to the attention of the domestic, or
pointing out Wragg to Adderley and Roebuck, demonstrates
their interdependence and insists upon it. If this is its function
at the present time, then criticism (which may appear to be secondary, merely repetitive) has at least a prima-facie case also to
be seen as primary. Or rather, the whole primary–secondary
relationship begins to seem ungroundable: perhaps there is, in
respect of the literature/criticism nexus, *no* primary, no resting
place, no home?

Mein Irisch Kind

If we were looking for an area of repression, in which unspeakable, *unheimlich* secrets recurrently haunt the *heimlich* texts of

British culture and prove to be their foundation as much as their undoing, the secondary that worryingly questions the standing of their primary, then we would do well to look slightly more closely at Matthew Arnold's account of the case of Wragg. The Victorian period broadly encouraged the operation of a complex system of social distinction which finally confined most of those determined as the 'lower' orders within the limits of what can be seen as a specific, unifying 'race'. The common characteristics supposedly shared by the labouring classes, Jews, southern Europeans and non-Europeans subjugated by empire included moral degeneracy and physical uncleanliness, and, in consequence, a systematic tendency towards desecration of the unified holy shrine of domesticity and hygiene. In Britain, any one instance of inferiority could readily be taken as a sign of the others and there are plenty of examples of a kind of 'network of affinities'[20] supporting a programme of racial totalisation that constructed foreigners – and the working class in general – as hovel-dwelling, bathroom-subverting, low-browed, dirty, cunning, dark-skinned 'savages'.

In Britain, one of the chief objects of this kind of derision was of course the Irish. As early as the mid seventeenth century, Irish servants who had been summarily shipped to service in the British West Indies were liable to establish common cause with black slaves in rebellions against their common masters.[21] By the nineteenth century the word 'Irish' functioned broadly in English as a term signifying the wild, intemperate, aggressive behaviour and illogical untutored argument deemed characteristic of dark-skinned savagery in general. That many of the poorest sections of Britain's industrial cities could be nominated 'Irishtown' or 'Irish Court' without demur is a telling detail in respect of the degrading, grubby context in which Arnold is at pains to locate Wragg:

> ...by the Ilissus there was no Wragg, poor thing! And 'our unrivalled happiness' – what an element of grimness, bareness, and hideousness mixes with it and blurs it; the workhouse, the dismal Mapperly Hills – how dismal those who have seen them will remember – the gloom, the smoke, the cold, the strangled illegitimate child! ... And the final touch – short, bleak, and inhuman: *Wragg is in custody.* The sex lost in the confusion of our unrivalled happiness; or

(shall I say) the superfluous Christian name lopped off by the straightforward vigour of our old Anglo-Saxon breed![22]

Wragg's context, involving dirt, labour, poverty, moral irresponsibility and the defilement of domesticity in the form of her illegitimate child and her infanticide, surely presents her in this sense not as Anglo-Saxon, but as something Anglo-Saxons have 'lopped off' in an attempt to dispose of it: as Irish, a representative of that ubiquitous, emasculated, and by now thoroughly 'feminised' Celtic culture whose apparent nature Arnold, in his writings elsewhere, had done much to characterise.[23] We need make nothing of the fact that not five miles from the dismal Mapperley Hills (how dismal those who have seen them will remember) the map shows a quite separate, 'lopped off' town called – exquisitely – Arnold. For Wragg's anarchic, anti-patriarchal, *unheimlich* eruption in Arnold's text as the Other, repressed by a self-satisfied Anglo-Saxon bourgeois and colonial ideology, invites us by its own force to see her as a version of an immemorial displaced figure. It is one that, despite the demands of and for Home (Ireland's claims for 'Home' Rule climax in 1870, with the founding of the Home Rule movement), seems forever doomed to wander homelessly in the English psyche:

> *Frisch weht der Wind*
> *Der Heimat zu*
> *Mein Irisch Kind*
> *Wo weilest du?*

That these lines, for English speakers, urge a return to Eliot as much as to Wagner is not accidental. *The Waste Land*'s use of the sailor's song from *Tristan und Isolde* is a significant part of the poem's focus upon wandering, rootlessness and homelessness as a feature of the Western experience in the twentieth century. And when we return to Eliot's essay 'The Function of Criticism', his diatribe against the 'inner voice' seems to spring from similar concerns. The central objection to the 'inner voice' is that it is exclusive. If its presence defines true Englishness, in a sense that *Heimat* points to, then its absence must bar the American Eliot from that company, however successful had been his elocutionary exertions over the years in sedulous pursuit of the English 'outer voice'.

Eliot's overriding critical notion was always of an adjustable 'order' or tradition of truly great Western writers, in which the advent of newcomers made a regular realignment necessary: the 'outsider' is thus accommodated, domesticated, put in place and made 'at home'. Eliot's progress towards conversion to the established church starts after the publication of *The Waste Land* and perhaps represents, as Edward Said has suggested, a turning away from the difficulties of *filiation* (natural continuity between generations: something prohibited by his exile and the difficulties of his marriage to Vivienne Haigh) and towards the alternative involvements available through *affiliation*, that is the bondings offered by 'institutions, associations and communities'.[24] This would certainly encourage a sense of the weaving of the individual talent into the web of connections afforded by the great Western tradition, so that an inherited American, Republican and Protestant commitment might eventually be transformed into the infamous English affiliative trio of Royalism, Classicism and Anglo-Catholicism.

Natural justice suggests that the strenuous pursuit of such strange Gods should be rewarded by a modicum of acceptance. Eliot's uncomprehending resentment when the 'inner voice' of Englishness turns out to be vested elsewhere is correspondingly acute. Its monument is the sudden eruption into the text of 'The Function of Criticism' – garnished for better effect with a broad range of modernist poetic devices – of that over-full railway carriage, whose denizens can be derided for asserting their insufferably boistrous, fully affiliated Englishness as football supporters on a trip to foreign parts at the expense of the exclusion from their number of a would-be fellow-traveller.

Most Europeans will of course be uncomfortably aware of the phenomenon of football as the focus of riotous affiliative nationalism in the twentieth and twenty-first centuries. In this, as in other regards, the United States retains an unviolated innocence and Eliot's American experience can hardly have prepared him for behaviour of this sort. That perhaps confirms – despite his best efforts at Anglicisation – how American he had remained. By their football supporters shall ye know them, and indeed it seems to have been precisely by those means that his discovery is made of an *unheimlich* spectre of exclusion located at the very heart of the English *heimlich*. What could offer to be more *heimlich* for a Harvard-educated traveller in pursuit of the great Western tradition than a seat in a carriage of the Great Western Railway?

The eruption that confronts Eliot in that carriage is a phenomenon for which the British have a particular and revealing term: *hooliganism*. The provenance of the word 'hooligan' is clear, disturbing, and once more involves nomenclature. It probably derives from an account (published in 1899) of the exploits of a fictitious denizen of Irish Court in East London called 'Patrick Hooligan'.[25] In short, 'hooligan' carries the clear connotation 'Irish'. It offers a classic displacement of violent disorderly behaviour onto a despised and supposedly 'savage' subculture, with the implication that it is racially characteristic. Throughout the twentieth century, the increasingly broad deployment of the term in Britain has been part of a series of complex ideological manoeuvres by which the British have tried to negotiate an engagement with what they still presume to call the 'Irish problem' – that is, by writing off the activities of an anti-colonial movement as the typical behaviour of degraded barbarians. That the rise in what is now firmly perceived and routinely denounced as 'football hooliganism' in Britain increasingly parallels the rise of violent rejection of British rule in parts of Ireland no doubt warrants further investigation in these terms.

Of course, from time immemorial there has been a tradition in Britain and throughout Europe of carnivalesque behaviour which, with its riotous upturning of accepted values and hierarchies, its commitment to 'rough music' and the crude extralegal settling of scores, has appeared to override civil authority and has sometimes fostered serious political challenge to it. More recently in Britain there has been a tradition of rowdy, law-breaking behaviour that – if practised by, say, undergraduates at the 'older' universities – could be safely written off as 'high spirits', or part of the tradition of the undergraduate 'Rag'. But this kind of boisterousness has increasingly – once it is seen to attract lesser breeds without the law – invited the moralising tendencies of magistrates and others as a prelude to its denunciation as the work of 'football hooligans'.

The brief but memorable eruption of football hooliganism into Eliot's 'The Function of Criticism' is a matter of some moment then; not least because it resonates with the eruption in Matthew Arnold's 'The Function of Criticism' of a similar, violently disorderly force. Linked to Eliot's not only by a potential Irish dimension, but by a name – Wragg – in which, as Arnold (quintessentially an Oxford Man) would know, the spectre of youthful disruptive behaviour also lurks – this side of Ionia, Attica and the Ilissus at least – it stands as a factor with which British culture, and its literary criticism, has had to come to terms.

First Aid For The Choking Victim

However, at what Foucault calls the 'preconceptual' level, Arnold's essay and Eliot's perhaps share much more extensive common ground. Together they tell us a good deal about the ideological freight carried by literary criticism at the moment of its installation as a key component of Anglo-American culture. Both promote and reinforce a fundamental division between the 'domestic' and the 'foreign', between 'home' and 'away', 'us' and 'them', in which the complexities surrounding the *heimlich* are actively at work. For Arnold, 'foreignness' involves the 'free play of ideas', which can only influence for the good an English insularity committed to the merely practical. For Eliot, the 'foreign' offers an ordered, hierarchical stability to shore against what he sees as the disorder likely to flow from the chaotic and potentially revolutionary English 'inner voice' on which John Middleton Murry and later D.H. Lawrence seem to insist.

Of course, that is only the crudest sketch of the terrain in question, but in general terms it seems to confirm that the subject position offered by both examples of this discourse – and I am taking Arnold's and Eliot's essays as crucially definitive locations and formulations of a discourse that will for a generation supply the common coin of academic literary criticism in the English-speaking world – systematically presents the critic in terms of a voice of sophisticated 'foreignness': a piece of equipment central to the cool appraising stance of the outsider. Coleridge's notion of a praetorian cadre of teachers operating within society as a select 'clerisy', or Arnold's idea of the recruitment of an elite fifth column of trained academic 'aliens', comes disturbingly to mind. The Arnold-influenced *Newbolt Report* (1921), direct precursor in Britain of professionalised academic literary criticism, speaks chillingly of university teachers of English as 'missionaries'.

Of course, Arnold professes sympathy for Wragg whilst Eliot maintains a frigid scorn for the possessors of the 'inner voice'. But both accept – as colonising outsiders who claim to be able to see what the savage aboriginal insiders cannot – the necessity of recognising the paradoxical Englishness of each eruption. Eliot's essay is important because it sanctions the transfer of aspects of its own eruption to Arnold's and establishes a resonance – albeit deeply submerged – with the case of Wragg. Freud's point is confirmed in both: the *unheimlich* represents a repressed dimension of the *heimlich*. Meanwhile, the links of football hooliganism with an older tradition of Carnival, and even the 'psychological ono-matopoeia' of Wragg's name (of which Arnold as we have seen makes a great deal), begin to hint at a sanctioned loosening of moral strictures. And that disturbing prospect starts, darkly, and surprisingly, to suggest the Mapperley Hills and Paddington Station as unlikely locations of a long-hidden and unified *unheim-lich* with which literary criticism, at its academic inception in Britain, feels it has somehow to engage.

In short, I am suggesting that the essays of Arnold and Eliot cohere around the eruptions of this Wragg–Hooligan nexus. Its vague roots lie, I would also suggest, in a forgotten – or repressed – dimension of British culture. In proposing its consideration as a single unit, I do so with only residual misgivings about the reduction and false clarity this imposes on its shadowy complexity. It is hardly counter-intuitive, after all, to suggest that the *unheimlich* lying within the *heimlich* in the modern British psyche has something to do with Ireland. And this is no more than to say that Ireland can always be perceived by an inherent prejudice as the Anarchy to a Culture whose presuppositions (like those of 'Britain' itself) are and always have been English.

What confronts both Arnold and Eliot, as they consider the function of literary criticism in its postindustrial setting, is thus the stirring of a pre-industrial ghost: a wholly disconcerting prospect in which that which is 'away' in football terms star-tlingly erupts into that which is 'home'. As missionaries, their project is nothing less than the imposition of a law and order on this savage chaos. Their central aim is to 'map' it, to establish the contours of 'home', by imposing an appellation that we have perhaps for too long endorsed: *English*. As part of the process, both offer to speak on behalf of a complex and hitherto covert but none the less authentic *Englishness*, an *inside*, which apparently reluctantly agrees to emerge in order to take on the policing role of *outside*. But by the stratagem of backing thus humbly into the limelight, 'authentic' Englishness – Wragg, the absurd claims of the 'inner voice' – manages to obscure something far more radical, far more deeply 'inside' and implicated with itself. In calling up this deep-seated internal challenge to the law and order of English literary criticism and nominating it, however rawly, as 'Irish', I suppose I am finally trying to outline a principle that out-Arnolds Arnold and out-Eliots Eliot: one that challenges fundamental English presuppositions in the most fundamental way; that ultimately refuses their very logic, their very ordering of the world, their very notion of causality, of the plausible in scholarship, the very oppositions on which this depends, and that refuses in the end the distinction between 'literature' and 'criticism', and between those modes of 'primary' and 'secondary' on which – as in Arnold and Eliot – it apparently insists.

The voice that has most relentlessly made this challenge over the years is inevitably an Irish one. It is that of Oscar Wilde. It speaks most cogently in the essay that presents his astonishing reply to Arnold and, as it were in advance, to Eliot: 'The Critic as Artist' (1891). In effect, what this essay awards to criticism is a primary not a secondary role:

> Without the critical faculty, there is no artistic creation at all, worthy of the name ... criticism demands infinitely more cultivation than creation does... Anybody can write a three volumed novel. It merely requires a complete ignorance of both life and literature ... criticism is itself an art... It is to criticism that the future belongs... There was never a time when criticism was more needed than it is now. It is only by its means that Humanity can become conscious of the point at which it has arrived.[26]

The work of a true – albeit dandified – hooligan, this polemic effortlessly reverses the apparently immutable hierarchy identified by Foucault, just as Wilde's whole life from the level of a paradoxical literary style to that of a committed sexual role seems to have been geared to the reversal at all levels and in all respects of the English sense of how things are and should be. 'Considered as an instrument of thought,' he writes, 'the English mind is coarse and undeveloped. The only thing that can purify it is the growth of the critical instinct.'[27] For reversals on that scale, of course, he paid the price that hooligans pay.

The principle at stake may nevertheless be allowed finally to challenge the notion of mere repetition that lies at the heart of traditional ideas of literary criticism, certainly in its profession-alised form in the academy. I hope to have suggested that a different notion of repetition might finally engage us, and will develop this idea in a later chapter. It is one whose aim is the generation of the new in terms of the only kind of newness we can recognise because its source is the old. I have in mind a criticism not merely anxious to raise the spectre of the *unheimlich*, but also intent, not on nullifying it, but on somehow including and promoting it within the material it examines – indeed of openly scrutinising those elements that its initial impulse is to try to occlude or swallow. When such a criticism then takes the literary analysis of the past as its raw material, puts Arnold and Eliot's criticism, that is, on the syllabus, with a standing equal to that of their so-called 'creative' writing, it will be releasing repetition from its servitude to precedence, and presenting it as a vital source of the new.

What we can retain from Foucault is surely the notion that, as part of the project of modernity, the essence of a truly modern criticism will not involve the reinforcement of so-called transcendental standards or structures, or any of the other lineaments of a tired, not to say oppressive, scholarly tradition. It will rather call for a kind of principled and self-inventing betrayal of that tradition whose investigation of criticism's own presuppositions will wilfully promote what are, by traditional standards, bogus connections and parallels of the sort that I have been shamelessly deploying: their aim an expansion of the possibilities of our *use* of criticism as a material intervention into history, rather than the prosecution of what we misguidedly think of as scholarly 'facts' or 'truth'.

Such a project absolves criticism from any commitment to the tetchy pursuit of true judgement or, worse, the soul-gelding aridity of *quellenforschung* (investigation of sources). Instead it turns into a creative genre in its own right; one whose fundamental mode is a sort of pre-emptive repetition: a matter (I begin, I dare say, to sound 'Irish') of getting the repetition in first: its central feature the active identifying, confronting and *using* of the *unheimlich*, the pressing home of Freud's deconstructive proposal that the *unheimlich* is in some way or other a sub-species of the *heimlich*, until those positions are virtually reversed. Until, that is, the *heimlich* appears almost as a sub-species of the *unheimlich*, and we begin to face the possibility that 'home' is only the tamed and taming doll's house we construct as a poor bulwark against the apparitions that permanently haunt us.

That the various rooms of one's home may be comfortably lined with books, plays and poems perhaps only intensifies an unease that lies at the heart of that vision of domesticity. And perhaps it serves finally to confront us with a prospect that is genuinely frightening because truly known of old and, though long repressed, long familiar: the appalling possibility that home is where the art is: that, in terms of the *unheimlich* critical vision, what we think of as home and what we think of as art are in some way shockingly coterminous in their role as mere vehicles for the most paltry of human comforts.

It is a view whose implications have undergone a crucial probing in those numerous voices that have spoken and continue to speak of the homelessness, expropriation, expatriation and exile that remain central features of life in our time. The range is vast, and perhaps the case of Wragg, for whom custody clearly stands in a deeply ironic opposition to the 'home' that would have prevented her crime, lies at one end of it. At the other, a hundred years, two world wars, revolutions and holocausts on, lies the work of Theodor Adorno. His judgement that 'Dwelling, in the proper sense, is now impossible. The traditional residences we grew up in have grown intolerable' concludes, at its uttermost, bitter reach, that 'Today ... it is part of morality not to be at home in one's home'[28]

In respect of art, the sort of homeless, 'hooligan' criticism I am advocating must eventually subscribe to a morality of that sort. And if uncomplicated notions of universality and transcendence serve only to mask the specificity of our present, a criticism more responsive to its opportunities (or demands) must be one whose roots in and connections with the here and the now are fully and actively sought, deliberately foregrounded, exploited as a first principle. It's a critical stance that has recently attracted a rather clumsy, but distinctive name: presentism. A presentist criticism's engagement with the text takes place precisely in terms of those dimensions of the modern world that most ringingly chime – perhaps as ends to its beginnings – with the events of the past. Its centre of gravity is accordingly 'now', rather than 'then'. Of course, a bland, unthinking confidence that the contours of the past will neatly match those of our own day – a view effectively skewered by those historians' gibes that employ 'presentism' as a term of disapprobation – is not in question. A newly committed, self-consciously 'presentist' literary criticism stands as something of quite a different order, particularly – as subsequent chapters of this book will seek to show – when it focuses on work that is already assumed to have a degree of current cultural centrality, such as the plays of Shakespeare. Its project is scrupulously to seek out salient aspects of the present as a crucial trigger for its investigations. Reversing, to some degree, the stratagems of new historicism, it deliberately begins with the material present and allows that to set its interrogative agenda. Perhaps this simply makes overt what covertly happens anyway. In principle, it involves the fundamentally radical act of putting one's cards on the table. In practice, as the following specific examples aim to demonstrate, it calls for a heightened degree of critical self-awareness.

And if it is finally able to plumb the deepest entrails of a culture, beyond the level at which any way of life feels itself to be 'at home', bringing to the surface – or, better, bringing the surface down to – whatever inhibits that culture's genuine nourishment, then such a criticism may aptly, and in the name of a more beneficial notion of eruption, be finally linked to a strategy whose simple design seems, astonishingly, to be outlined on the walls of every American restaurant. For there, in that most portentous of modern locations, an exotic rubric suddenly and darkly speaks of 'First Aid For The Choking Victim'.

Central to the welfare of any Choking Victim (and surely most of us will from time to time have felt included in that company) is the principle that there is a sort of eruption which can be good for you, and that in its most benign form – that of regurgitation – lies the basis of a new beginning. In the circumstances, and to mention nomenclature for the last time, it strikes me as only slightly uncanny that the name given to this most radical of critical gambits happens to be 'The Heimlich Manoeuvre'.

3
Bryn Glas

A French connection?

It has been rightly observed that, half-way down the cat's throat, any self-respecting mouse ought at least to consider saying a few words about 'us cats'. For similar reasons, perhaps an essay entitled 'Bryn Glas' ought at least to consider saying a few words about Jacques Derrida's work called *Glas*. That dismaying celebration of the relationship between texts confronts the reader with two parallel columns of print. On the left-hand side, the philosopher Hegel engages in a rational analysis of the concept of the family, the Law and the State. Meanwhile, on the right, the text cites and discusses the writings of a notorious thief, homosexual and transvestite – Jean Genet – along with passages about matters such as proper names, signatures, onomatopoeia and the process of signification at large. The mode of negotiation between the columns becomes, of course, a crucial factor.

Texts, Derrida's strategy implies, speak with no single, privileged voice but with one that owes due homage to the work of other texts always covertly juxtaposed with, inserted into, or grafted upon them. In *Glas*, one kind of rationality – Hegel's –

literally confronts, even glares at, its opposite, that of Genet: yet, curiously, the one also seems to be shaped by, and finally almost dependent upon, the other. What first appears as a radical disjunction between the two columns turns gradually into a kind of fruitful connection, something that plunges the very notion of 'text' into a revealing crisis, exposing and bringing into question the process of 'smoothing over the joins' in which our production of meaning has such a massive investment. This chapter's focus is on that process, and thus on a boundary, a frontier, a 'join' that needs to be smoothed over or dissolved before the texts on either side of it can inherit the coherence to which both lay claim. With the upholders of reason and law on the one side, and with thieves and subversives on the other, that text – to this day – is called 'Great Britain'.

Blue remembered hills

In fact, the title 'Bryn Glas' draws on one of the languages of Britain. The words are Welsh, and if English is the vehicle of reason and the law then they belong very much in the opposite column. The English rhyme 'Taffy was a Welshman, Taffy was a thief' makes no bones about that. An English perception of the world traditionally imposes a specific sanction on the outlandish Celtic hordes: brisk exclusion from civilisation as we know it. The very word 'Welsh' derives from the Old English *wælisc*, meaning, brutally and dismissively, 'foreign'.

Bryn Glas is the name of a place in Wales. 'Bryn' means hill. 'Glas' means blue. The Blue Hill. However, there is a slight complication, which perhaps reinforces some English suspicions about the Welsh capacity for undermining reason and logic, for 'Glas' can mean 'green' as well as 'blue'. What English presents as a clear distinction, Welsh refuses, and, dividing the spectrum slightly differently, confirms its foreignness by challenging a whole view of the world. Nevertheless, in translation, both sorts of hill, blue or green, seem happily to incline towards the other column on the page, where a kind of quintessential Englishness awaits them. 'There is a Green Hill far away' begins a famous nineteenth-century hymn about a carefully Anglicised Jerusalem, its chords evocative, in males of my generation, of nothing more challenging than school

uniforms, morning assembly, and a gossamer guilt gently
yoking football field and bicycle shed. Perhaps more poignant
is A.E. Housman's secular hymn to an irrecoverable past,
recorded in *A Shropshire Lad*:

> Into my heart an air that kills
> From yon far country blows.
> What are those blue remembered hills,
> What spires, what farms are those?
>
> That is the land of lost content,
> I see it shining plain,
> The happy highways where I went
> And cannot come again.
>
> (*A Shropshire Lad* xl)

Border country

Nevertheless, Bryn Glas remains an actual place concretely and,
in view of the ambiguity of its hue, appropriately located in
Wales. It lies just inside the Welsh border, a few miles below
Knighton, to the west of a small settlement called Pilleth. In
fact, Housman's English vision turns out to be rather acute.
Bryn Glas, the Blue Hill, lies only a few miles from Ludlow, the
setting of *A Shropshire Lad*.

Whether this signals Wales as that 'land of lost content' must
remain a moot point. At first sight, in historical terms, 'content'
seems the last prospect that such a country might offer to
English eyes. As England's next-door neighbour, indeed as
holder of the dubious distinction of being England's first
colony, Wales inherits a history of constant and often violent
penetration of its borders. The result is a duality of experience
and commitment which to this day makes the Principality virtually ungraspable as a single, unified entity. At least two distinct
'readings' of it are always available, one Welsh and one English,
and the different texts each of them generates are worryingly
co-terminous: they occupy the same page. As a result, shadowing the picture drawn and framed by laws administered from its
Anglicised towns and cities, another, ghostlier, Wales of poets,
minstrels and prophets 'apprenticed in ancient lore' has always
beckoned its inhabitants, well beyond the English ken.[1]

That clash between 'law' and 'lore' appears invariably to characterise the experience of colonist and colonised in Wales. At the heart of a culture obsessed by genealogy, blood-descent and complex, carefully nurtured family relations, the serpentine character of Welsh kinship structures seems destined – if not designed – to undermine linear English certainties, both legal and constitutional. The major political upheaval of the fourteenth century had, not inappropriately, climaxed in Wales. In the summer of 1399, the deposition of Richard II, the ultimate *de jure* monarch of the old medieval order, removed the last king of Britain to rule by undisputed hereditary right. No doubt the spectacle of Richard's scrambling *de facto* successors helped fan opportunistic flames of revolt in the Principality. An inherited fondness for grandiose titular claims (still mocked even in the twentieth century by Dylan Thomas's sobriquet 'The Rimbaud of Cwmdonkin Drive') probably helped.

When insurrection came, it certainly involved an eruption of that 'other', non-English Wales: a rising against law, in the name of lore, and to the clamant flourishing of a title. The revolt of Owain Glyn Dŵr, self-proclaimed Prince of Wales, effectively lasted, with fluctuations of intensity, from his assumption of the title on 6 September 1400 until the degeneration of his campaign into guerrilla warfare, and his decline into a desperate and hunted man, by 1409. At its height, an 'awesome Welsh army' was mustered in support of what might be termed a classic anti-colonialist project designed, in Glyn Dŵr's own words, to release Wales from 'the madness of the English barbarians'. Sustained by the prophecies of Merlin and Taliesin, it encouraged those Welsh who had felt exiles in their own land since the victories of Edward I to pursue claims made as the original 'Britons'. Glyn Dŵr had little trouble linking himself with a long line of Welsh 'Messiahs' or 'redeemers', including the fabled King Arthur, who offered to regain for their compatriots control of the whole island.[2]

The Battle of Britain

The climax came on 22 June 1402 and it came at Bryn Glas. There, at the head of his troops, Glyn Dŵr won his only major victory: over an English force led by Edmund Mortimer, uncle of the heir of the Earl of March. The bloodiness of the battle, in which the English were decimated and Mortimer captured, made it immediately memorable. The subsequent alleged mutilation of the bodies of the English dead by Welsh women brought legendary status. Later, in what amounted to a major public relations coup, the captured Mortimer defected and married Glyn Dŵr's daughter Catherine.

Most students of English have already encountered Bryn Glas, perhaps without realising it, through Shakespeare's version of the events at the beginning of *1 Henry IV*. The King's project for an expedition to the Holy Land has to be postponed owing to the sudden arrival of a 'post from Wales loaden with heavy news',

> Whose worst was that the noble Mortimer,
> Leading the men of Herefordshire to fight
> Against the irregular and wild Glendower,
> Was by the rude hands of that Welshman taken,
> A thousand of his people butchered,
> Upon whose dead corpse there was such misuse,
> Such beastly shameless transformation,
> By those Welshwomen done, as may not be
> Without much shame retold or spoken of.
>
> (1.1.34–46)

The source of the information is clearly Holinshed:

> Owen Glendouer, according to his accustomed manner, robbing and spoiling within the English borders, caused all the forces of the shire of Hereford to assemble togither against them, vnder the conduct of Edmund Mortimer earle of March. But coming to try the matter by battell, whether by treason or otherwise, so it fortuned, that the English power was discomfited, the earle taken prisoner, and aboue a thousand of his people slaine in the place. The shamefull villanie vsed by the Welshwomen towards the dead carcasses, was such, as honest eares would be ashamed to heare, and continent toongs to speake thereof.[3]

Glendower's 'irregular and wild' function clearly derives from this. But where does Shakespeare's more precise 'beastly

shameless transformation' come from? Its source is also Holinshed, where the cruelty of the Scythian Queen Tomyzis and of
Fulvia, wife of Mark Antony, is sternly denounced. Yet in
neither case, he says, is their cruelty

> comparable to this of the Welshwomen; which is worthie to
> be recorded to the shame of a sex pretending the title of
> weake vessels, and yet raging with such force of fiercenesse
> and barbarisme. For the dead bodies of the Englishmen,
> being above a thousand lieng upon the ground imbrued in
> theire owne blood, was a sight (a man would think)
> greevous to looke upon, and so farre from exciting and stir-
> ring up affections of crueltie; that it should rather have
> moued the beholders to commiseration and mercie: yet did
> the women of Wales cut off their priuities and put one part
> thereof into the mouths of euerie dead man, in such sort
> that the cullions hoong downe to their chins; and not so
> contented, they did cut off their noses and thrust them into
> their tailes as they laie on the ground mangled and defaced.
> This was a verie ignominious deed, and a woorsse not com-
> mitted among the barbarous: which though it make the
> reader to read it, and the hearer to heare it, ashamed: yet
> bicause it was a thing doone in open sight, and left testified
> in historie; I see little reason whie it should not be imparted
> in our mother toong to the knowledge of our owne countri-
> men, as well as unto strangers in a language unknowne.[4]

Certain features of this passage are worth noting:

1   The stress on female duplicity ('a sex pretending the title
     of weake vessels, and yet raging with such force of fierce-
     nesse and barbarisme') and its presentation as a central
     characteristic of an outlandish and destructive savagery
     plainly directed at – indeed hacking off – the fundamental
     indicator of native manhood.
2   The stress on the specific location of this unnatural force.
     It resides in 'Welshwomen', 'women of Wales', etc.
3   The stress on language. Despite the earlier judgement of
     the event's shamefully unspeakable nature, we now find it
     spoken of in meticulous detail, with a particularly pious
     commitment to English: 'I see little reason whie it should

not be imparted in our mother toong to the knowledge of our owne countrimen, as well as unto strangers in a language unknowne'. Clearly, the Welsh tongue – here the very badge of deceit and barbarism – must not be allowed to perform its savage, emasculating operations on English.

It's surely also clear that we are not here dealing with the transparent reporting of fact, but with something that, by the time Holinshed chronicled the issues, had come to bear complex cultural freight. Even if the mutilation of the bodies had been actual, some careful symbolic structuring is clearly at work in the narrative. A methodical routine of 'reversal' operates, whereby orifices are systematically stuffed with members from opposite regions. The upper region, the head, receives the penis; the lower region, the 'taile', receives the nose. In this process, men find themselves turned upside-down and inside-out by agents of a fundamental disorder, women, just as England is subverted by its foreign 'other', Wales. This, surely, is the wholesale inversion hinted at by Shakespeare's 'beastly . . . transformation'. If we wanted a *locus classicus* we would need to look no further than Ovid's *Metamorphoses*, or the story of the enchantress Circe.

The play goes some way towards confirming this reading in its subsequent portrayal of the power and implications of a traditional, magical and shape-shifting Welshness. Owen Glendower is a far more complex figure than the mere blowhard that English tradition, and Hotspur's well-known gibes, seek to endorse. The sparring between them probably tells us as much about Hotspur as about his adversary:

Glendower: I can call spirits from the vasty deep.
Hotspur: Why, so can I, or so can any man;
   But will they come when you do call for them?
                 (3.1.51–3)

None the less, enough Welsh princely blood genuinely ran in Glyn Dŵr's veins to lend a certain legitimacy to his title and to the revolt mounted in its name. He claimed descent, after all, from Llewellyn, the last native-born Prince of Wales. In his assumption of precisely that title, Glyn Dŵr ranks as a credible alternative to another, rather less authentic-sounding, incumbent who was also in the field: Henry of Monmouth, Shakespeare's Hal, invested by his father as Prince of Wales just twelve months before. Shakespeare's version of Hotspur's encounter with the 'great magician, damn'd Glendower' (1.3.82) obviously locks on to traditional oppositions that caricature both the Celtic sensibility and the Anglo-Saxon. The one, dealing in mythology, magic, prophecy and lore, duly rants, boasts and carries on in the face of the other's hard-headed commitment to reason, common sense and law. But, not unlike Derrida's *Glas*, the play goes on to blur the edges of exactly those distinctions.

Perhaps most important are the implications at work in its depiction of 'down-trod' Mortimer (1.3.133): for here an English hero-figure, a serious pretender to the English throne, 'proclaim'd / By Richard that dead is, the next of blood' (1.3.143–4), is kept wholly in thrall by the charms of a Welsh woman. Holinshed's sparse reference to her, 'daughter of the said Owen', is expanded in the play to create a far more disturbing figure who, Circe-like, seems easily able to subvert Mortimer's English manhood – certainly as measured by the standards of the absurdly leaping Hotspur. Significantly, her powers are clearly located in a language that Shakespeare never attempts to transliterate, but presumably hands over to the invention of Welsh-speaking actors working within the company. It is amply displayed. The stage directions indicate a completed interchange with her father '*Glendower speaks to her in Welsh, and she answers him in the same*' followed by three full speeches in which '*The lady speaks in Welsh*' (3.1.192–206), culminating in her singing of a '*Welsh song*' (3.1.238).

The strongly suasive powers of the language manifest themselves in Mortimer's response to it. Glendower's daughter is transformed almost into an embodiment of what she speaks: even her tears become 'that pretty Welsh / Which thou pourest down from these swelling heavens' (3.1.194–5). But the essential feature of the language appears in a more telling dimension, as a highly wrought 'effeminate' or 'femininising' capacity. An uncomprehending Mortimer comments,

> . . . thy tongue
> Makes Welsh as sweet as ditties highly penn'd,
> Sung by a fair queen in a summer's bow'r
> With ravishing division to her lute.
>
> (3.1.201–4)

– or in her father's translation,

> She bids you on the wanton rushes lay you down,
> And rest your gentle head upon her lap,
> And she will sing a song that pleaseth you,
> And on your eyelids crown the god of sleep,
> Charming your blood with pleasing heaviness,
> Making such difference 'twixt wake and sleep
> As is the difference betwixt day and night,
> The hour before the heavenly-harness'd team
> Begins his golden progress in the east.
>
> (3.1.207–15)

To stress as 'feminine' the narcotic aspect of Welsh, its capacity to create a 'bower of bliss' whose modes dissolve and transcend the male, order-giving boundaries of an English-speaking world, is to draw attention to the culture's larger, subversive, and in a complex sense 'effeminate' role in early modern Britain. Hotspur's 'manly' rejection of such charms 'I had rather hear Lady my brach howl in Irish' (3.1.230) not only reinforces the contrast, it neatly reminds the audience of that larger Celtic world that its own commitment to English and Englishness had long been trying to suppress.

Of course, that world had – and has – never altogether gone away. In fact, after the battle of Bosworth, Merlin's prophecies about the return of the Welsh hero-king to rule over the whole island of Britain almost seemed about to come true. Henry VII was certainly a Welshman. He packed his court with his countrymen, named his eldest son Arthur and took care to observe St David's day. As the lineaments of the Tudor dynasty unfolded, Welsh-speakers 'poured in' to London.[5]

However, when it came to the construction of a new entity called 'Britain', that massive ideological project which obsessed both the Tudors and Stuarts and on which the history plays focus with consuming intensity, Wales's fate would ultimately prove to be a matter more of incorporation than confederacy. As Gwyn A. Williams observes, 'A nation-state in formation was faced with the little local difficulty that there were actually two nations in it. One would have to be made invisible. So between 1536 and 1543, the English crown put through a series of measures which have gone down in Welsh history as the Act of Union.'[6]

The price of such 'union' was high. As a junior partner in what was to be virtually a new state, Wales had literally to be redefined. Firm borders and boundaries were imposed in the English mode. One result was that the city and county of Monmouth, unable to yield easily to such procedures, turned almost overnight into an anomaly; neither Welsh nor English, its newly invented indeterminacy persisted into the twentieth century. English became the only official language in Wales. Denied status as an authorised tongue, Welsh retreated to the hearth, the kitchen and the street.

To a considerable extent, the new self-confident and London-based Welsh were prepared to accede to such measures, in pursuit of what they saw as the greater prize – or the better pickings – offered by a coherent 'British' nation, and the sense of a complete, English-speaking 'world', separated from the rest of the globe, that it implied.[7] As Gwyn A. Williams puts it, 'An integrated Britain becomes visible first in a major migration of the Welsh to the centre of power.' London attracted 'all the exports, human and material, of the novel merchant capitalism' and the Welsh moved into 'every conceivable avenue of advancement', the process reaching its climax in the reign of Elizabeth I.[8] One direct result was the rise to prominence of Welsh families such as that of Dafydd Seisyllt, whose grandson became William Cecil, Elizabeth's key statesman, or indeed that of Morgan Williams, which three generations later produced Oliver Cromwell.[9]

Under Elizabeth, denounced by A.L. Rowse as 'that redheaded Welsh harridan', the 'remote and distinguished past' of the Welsh effectively made available – at least in influential intellectual terms – some sort of underpinning for the new national identity. Their very presence satisfactorily bore out claims for the ancient existence of that complete 'world', that independent Britishness, of which the Arthurian legends spoke. Geoffrey of Monmouth's *British History* swiftly became semi-official doctrine and Welsh scholars responded enthusiastically.[10] A London Welshman, John Dee, is even said to have coined the term 'British Empire'. Certainly, in addressing Elizabeth he styled himself 'hyr Brytish philosopher' and Dee's proposal of the Welshman Madoc as the discoverer of America 300 years before Columbus was seized on by a whole generation as a cultural and quasi-legal weapon against Spain.[11]

It may well be that an acquaintance with Welsh people in London accounts for Shakespeare's portrayal of Glendower as more sympathetic than his sources would encourage.[12] Obviously, his company contained at least two Welsh-speaking actors. This native Prince of Wales is certainly no babbling Caliban. He can, he tells us, speak English as well as Hotspur, having been 'train'd up in the English court' (3.1.116–17).[13] Nevertheless, his native Welsh must have inherited a disturbing role in an emerging British state whose interests lay in being monolingual. In the streets of London it would have stalked the English language like an importunate ghost. To most of those familiar with the major European tongues, Welsh would have seemed – as it still does – entirely exotic. In its written form, the apparent senseless conjunction of consonants generates blankness, if not bewilderment. In its spoken form, its requirement of unachievable phonemes, such as /ll/, mark it as impossibly alien, utterly estranging. As opaque to English ears as any African or Indian tongue – not that most Londoners would ever have encountered such rarities – it appeared to lack even the bare referentiality that Elizabethan popular culture was prepared to grant to the Romance languages or to Latin. The status of Welsh in Tudor London was completely different. Its apparent lack of even rudimentary transparency effectively marks it as totally outlandish. For English speakers, to hear Welsh is fundamentally disconcerting. In a sense it is to experience the alienating phenomenon of 'language' itself, as an unmediated, inexplicable, system of signs. It is to come face to face with an almost unacceptable 'given': the alarming and inextricable involvement of human beings in the sounds that they make with their mouths. It is to run full tilt into a material human world that seems wholly other. Worse, shockingly, it is one that claims rights to the same island.

The battle at Bryn Glas embodies this collision and offers some insight into Holinshed's anxiety over whether details of what happened should be made available through the medium of English. The importance of the events derives not only from the fact that they involved a decisive and brutal battle in which a large number of English were slaughtered by the Welsh. Shakespeare's play presents it as central to what might be called a genuine Battle of Britain. For in *1 Henry IV*, Bryn Glas and its consequences release that most disturbing of spectres: a militant feminine and femininising force, with a bloody knife in its hand, an incomprehensible tongue in its head, and with English manhood, the English language and (on both counts) English reality in its sights. When Welsh erupts onto the stage in that play, its evident complicity with an occluded but horribly violent reading of the past, present and future is what ensures its capacity to sap the claim of English to be the transparent, fully referential transmitter of a new-minted Britishness.[14]

Spirits from the vasty deep

The captive Mortimer's situation, unmanned – at least according to Hotspur – by a Welsh woman, undoubtedly echoes that of his hapless English comrades at Bryn Glas. However, the most potent wearer of that Circean mantle is perhaps located elsewhere. Falstaff is, of course, the play's most resourceful agent of 'beastly shameless transformation'. He has from the beginning nothing to do with the rational, daylight world with its distinctions and calibrations appropriate to truth, to law and to time (1.2.1–12). His bluster (2.4.164ff.) chimes easily with Glendower's

> . . . at my birth
> The front of heaven was full of fiery shapes,
> The goats ran from the mountains [etc.]
>   (3.1.34ff.)

– and meets the same hard-nosed response from Hal as Glendower's does from Hotspur. Indeed, Hal's and Hotspur's debunking 'English' rejection serves structurally to identify the reverberations of a submerged 'Welshness' that perhaps surprisingly turns out to link Falstaff and Glendower. Of course, they are already firmly yoked in other ways. Both have well-established connections with the Devil. Hal warns himself, in the guise of his father, that 'there is a devil haunts thee in the likeness of a fat old man ... Falstaff, that old white-bearded Satan' (2.4.441–57) and Falstaff himself speaks of 'that devil Glendower' (2.4.365). In fact, Glendower's command of 'spirits from the vasty deep' (3.1.50) presents itself as part of a Welsh repertoire which, as he proposes to Hotspur, 'can teach you, cousin to command the devil' (3.1.53). Such 'skimble-skamble stuff' includes, to Hotspur's disgust, '...reckoning upon the several devils' names/That were his lackeys' (3.1.151–2) so that his conclusion that 'the devil understands Welsh' (3.1.224) comes as no surprise.[15]

It is therefore not altogether unfitting that an element of disintegrative 'effeminacy' characterises Falstaff, reinforced when set against the background of a 'manly' unity which will form the basis of the emerging British state. Alan Sinfield makes the point explicitly: 'Falstaff represents in part effeminate devotion to women ... above all, with his drinking, eating, jesting, and fatness, Falstaff embodies unmasculine *relaxation* – loosening, softening, languishing, letting go etc.'[16] We can add that a final and betraying dimension of 'Welshness' accrues to Falstaff as a result of his suppressed links with Sir John Old-castle (*c.*1378–1417).[17] Falstaff's 'remote original', as the Arden editor calls him, was a High Sheriff of Herefordshire who became Lord Cobham by marriage in 1409. A friend of young Henry, Holinshed calls him a 'valiant captaine and a hardie gentleman', who was 'highly in the king's favour'. However, Henry casts him off when he is charged with Wycliffite heresy (Lollardism) and condemned. Escaping from the Tower, Oldcastle took refuge in Wales, where his presence served to underline the Principality's notorious and continuing potential for upheaval. Owain Glyn Dŵr's revolt may have been petering out, but a continuing Welsh disaffection could always be exploited by enemies of the English crown, and Oldcastle was thought to have been in contact with Glyn Dŵr's son.[18]

As a Welsh Circe, one whose brand of effeminacy is well capable of suborning the role of 'Prince of Wales', even down to mimicking it at one memorable point, Falstaff's banishment from the new united 'manly' Britain is inevitable. It provokes the official Prince of Wales's ruthless and appropriately 'English' rejection. It is one – to probe the effect of Falstaff's 'effeminacy' once more – whose words deliberately invert the performative utterances of marriage by locating them in the context of a momentous divorce: 'I do, I will' (2.4.475).

God for Harry

The unappeased spectre of a subverting, transforming and un-manning Wales haunts the rest of the tetralogy. *1 Henry IV* con-cludes with Henry's commitment to continue 'To fight with Glendower and the Earl of March' (5.5.40), but the play's second part presents Welshness in a more dangerously diffused mode. Falstaff remains 'in the devil's book' (2.2.43–4) along with Poins, and his 'effeminacy' continues, but in a sour, less ebullient vein. He dwindles, in his own depiction of himself and his page, into 'a sow that hath overwhelmed all her litter but one' (1.2.10–11), and his prospective rejection acquires nuances that present him precisely in terms of an outlandish, opaque language whose threat to the supremacy of English must be met by domestication:

> The Prince but studies his companions
> Like a strange tongue, wherein, to gain the language,
> 'Tis needful that the most immodest word
> Be look'd upon and learnt.
>
> (4.4.68–71)

A play apparently promoting the idea of a united 'British' state must obviously try to shoe-horn untidy exoticisms into a mode in which they can be appropriated to suit the central project.[19] *Henry V* begins with a sifting of the problems of the Salic law (which prohibited women from succeeding to the throne in parts of Europe) in pursuit of a firmer grip on the range and disposition of female power. Welshness duly appears in a differ-ent key. Falstaff and the subversive, 'effeminate', emasculating dimension he represents are notably absent: indeed the fat Knight has returned to the bosom of one of the great Welsh heroes, Arthur (2.3.9–10). The challenge to English has receded: its militant ascendancy can afford to allow that French is sufficiently referential to be joked at and with: even Pistol is able to mangle it sufficiently to produce a knowing humour (2.1.72). After all, foreign cultures valuably determine our own. We are what we oppose, and a 'fair and lucky war' may not unreasonably be mounted against any country prepared to square up to – and so define – the oncoming multicultural British force as simply 'the English' (2.4.1). That, to speak broadly, is what the French (and, latterly, foreign cultures at large) are traditionally for.

In fact, Englishness receives its final polishing in this play and enlistment in that crudely engrossing concept is repeatedly urged on and required of the army that Henry leads. Appropriating Scottishness, Irishness and Welshness, its project can be said to present itself, not as a set of distinctive cultural and linguistic features, so much as a kind of fundamental 'reality' that underlies sophisticated notions of difference. It constitutes the basis of that complete and discrete 'world', that the 'British' project set out to create. To be 'English', and a participant in that world, is thus, by this light, simply to be human. So the English spokesman in France sees 'French' possessions as the mere trappings of a massive pretension, and, speaking for the English King, urges his French 'brother'

> That you divest yourself and lay apart
> The borrowed glories that by gift of heaven,
> By law of nature and of nations, longs
> To him and his heirs...
> 　　　　　　　　　　　　　　　...resign
> Your crown and kingdom indirectly held
>
> From him the native and true challenger.
> 　　　　　　　　　　　(2.4.78–95)

This sense of being the final, fundamental reality, 'native and true', then becomes the licence for a broad process of Anglicisation, which the play duly chronicles: undertaken, not in the spirit of imposing a particular culture on one that pre-exists it, so much as discovering, and laying bare, a substratum that another competing and outlandish way of life has needlessly and mischievously obscured. There isn't much doubt that an Englishman, a 'plain soldier . . . a fellow of plain and uncoined constancy' as Henry V styles himself when wooing Katherine (5.2.150–5), with his 'poor and starved band' (4.2.15) of 'warriors for the working-day' (4.3.109) is going to prove superior to any effete and pretentious enemy.

The notion that a genuine nuts-and-bolts reality is discoverable beneath an obscuring complex veil that must, in the name of humanity, be plucked from it, gains increasing momentum in the plays. It underlies Hal's claim that his youthful excesses merely cloud a simple honesty that will subsequently appear. His later kingly penchant for disguising his true status and mingling with the soldiers before Agincourt, only triumphantly to reveal himself after the battle, springs from the same source. The construction of 'England' and Englishness as the model of that grounding reality becomes a major concern. Whenever another culture emerges, as French does through the use of its language, its fortifications prove readily piercable by honest English eyes. Either simple sniggering about names for parts of the body will suffice (3.4) or, as in the case of Pistol and his prisoner (4.4) the opacities of the language yield readily to a more knowing humour. English, the language of the 'real' world, is well able to penetrate and control foreignness simply because a palpable, homespun 'English' truth lies beneath everything. The claim made for a conquering Englishness is thus that it represents, not a specific, but a general situation: that it is acting on behalf, not of a particular regime, but of nothing less than the unsullied human condition itself. It brings, not subservience to an 'English' way of life, but the arrangement offered initially to the Welsh by the Acts of Union. This construction of the world as a kind of enormous *Anglia irredenta*, an England waiting to be reclaimed, allows, even encourages, those claims to unadorned foundational status that, in the last analysis, show through as what we are always tempted to call 'human nature'. If everyone, under the surface, is really like us, that is English, then to claim simply to be English is to present oneself as pristine, unsullied, unwarped and real. Other people have identifiable cultures and distinctive languages; in the 'land of lost content' we simply live, we simply speak, and we do so with immediate and transparent reference to the true, English-speaking world. Like Adam, in this 'other Eden' (*Richard II*, 2.1.42), we simply name.

Big name

However, as Derrida is at pains to point out, in *Glas* and elsewhere, Adam's project must be doomed to failure. A proper name ought indeed to involve pure reference, but since it is part of language it works like language, and always retains, willy-nilly, the capacity to signify.[20] This principle obviously works even more powerfully as one language crosses the border of another and engages in the process by which, as we put it in English, names come to be 'Anglicised'. Colonisation provides numberless rich examples of this process, each 'Englished' phoneme containing a miniature history of expropriation. In Wales, names traditionally indicated lineage and place of origin. The Acts of Union imposed the English concept of 'surname' on the Welsh, partly out of irritation, and partly as a symbol and symptom of incorporation.[21]

The name 'Owen Glendower', as Shakespeare gives it, offers a poignant example. Over and above its claim to refer to a distinct, placeless individual, its Anglicised form – which systematically elides links of blood and soil – signifies incursion, defeat and expropriation exactly to the degree that it is not Owain Glyn Dŵr. That name, with its Welsh luggage of signs invoking kinship, terrain, political commitment and history, lacks any of the transparency that English may mistakenly try to attribute to, or indeed, in characteristic gesture, to uncover in, 'Owen Glendower'. But the nature of Owain Glyn Dŵr's revolutionary project made his lineage and his connection with Welsh soil indispensable to him. It constituted 'the validating charter of his identity and of his claim'.[22] This kind of blood-and-soil link underwrites his claim to be the true Prince of Wales. The other Prince of Wales's roots – those of Hal – lie much less securely and indeed most significantly in Monmouth: to this day, as has been said, still thought of as border country.

Many names in these plays seem in fact to point to borders. Some of them do so directly because they have evidently crossed the border between one culture and another. Others hint at political borders whose crossing has provoked change. We have already noticed that the play contains vestigial reminders that Falstaff was originally named Oldcastle. A canny deployment of diminutives also operates, dragging a name across the border between formal and informal, often in a political cause. The French Princess Katherine rapidly dwindles to 'Kate' as part of the domesticating Anglicising process already noted. Indeed, at a telling moment, after chugging through a ludicrous array of French formal titles –

Up, princes, and with sword of honour edged
More sharper than your swords hie to the field.
Charles Delabreth, High Constable of France,
You Dukes of Orleans, Bourbon and of Berry,
Alençon, Brabant, Bar and Burgundy,
Jacques Chatillon, Rambures, Vaudemont,
Beaumont, Grandpré, Roussi and Fauconbridge,
Foix, Lestrelles, Boucicault and Charolais [etc.]

– the French King finds himself urging these worthies
against the mere, but significantly named, 'Harry England'
(3.5.38–48).

Pig time

None the less, a degree of insecurity hovers around this enterprise, and the playtext records its inescapable and worrying
presence. An important location of the attendant stresses is the
Welshman who enters right in the middle of *Henry V* (3.2). To
English eyes, Fluellen could not be more Welsh. Yet he could
also not be more acceptable or engaging. Anglicisation could
wish for no better advertisement. Although, as Gwyn A.
Williams has said, his father would probably have supported
Owain Glyn Dŵr, Fluellen's commitment to the English, or
rather British, project seems, at first sight, absolute.[23] His comic
pride in his nationality seems even to be fulfilled by that.
Indeed, he delights in confirming King Henry's own twice-
proclaimed, but still shady, Welshness (4.1.52, 4.7.104). And
although his loquaciousness carries more than an echo of
Glendower's, his ebullience and wholehearted loyalty prove
redemptive and reassuring. Praised for his 'care and valour'
(4.1.85), he can never be imagined mutilating the body of an
enemy. His commitment to those quaint provisions, the 'disci-
plines' of war, would certainly preclude such an action and his
concern to school his colleagues in the value of such prescriptions, as well as his readiness to berate the foreigners for their
ignorance of them, are memorable. He virtually embodies law
and order and fully supports the hanging of Bardolph for theft.
This is no devil, no monster, but a leek-wearing patriot, vigor-
ous and bustling in the service of his king. As a crowning virtue,
he speaks no word of Welsh.

Fluellen, in short, appears to be the model Welshman necessary to the project of a united Britain. However, there are complications. The first, since we have spoken of names, arises with
Fluellen's. The Folio confirms this as a heavily Anglicised
version of 'Llewellyn'. Llewellyn is not, of course, just any
Welsh name. All such – as we have seen – trail their own clouds
of glory, but this name can claim archetypal status. Llewellyn is
the name of the last native Prince of Wales (Llewellyn yr Olaf,
Llewellyn the last). Moreover, fittingly, and notoriously for
English ears, it deploys in full fig that distinctive phoneme
/ll/mentioned above, whose accurate pronunciation is a major
Welsh shibboleth.[24] Here, immediately recognisable to both
Welsh and English ears, is a distinctive sign of Welshness.
However, the initial, side-stepping and entirely Anglicised
phoneme embodied in 'Fluellen' signifies a language – and a
highly significant name – crudely enlisted and in the process
brutally reduced. Even more clearly than in the case of 'Owen
Glendower', in Fluellen's name a maimed linguistic ghost stirs,
rattles its English cage, and hints darkly at things that are now
literally unspeakable.

Just as Welshness finds itself determinedly Anglicised in
Fluellen, the English he speaks is no less heavily inflected, contorted and 'Welshified' to the satisfaction of English ears by the
use of standard parodic devices: the repetition of phrases such as
'look you' and confusion over the plurality of nouns ('leeks is
good' (5.1.59), etc.) Comically, endearingly – reassuringly – the
phoneme /b/ is consistently, to English ears, replaceable by /p/:

> the French is gone off, look you, and there is gallant and
> most prave passages. Marry, th'athversary was have posses-
> sion of the pridge, but he is enforced to retire, and the
> Duke of Exeter is master of the pridge. I can tell your
> majesty, the Duke is a prave man.
>
> (3.6.90ff.)

Droll, no doubt. But then, momentarily, the process starts to
backfire. Henry's plain, soldierly gallantry, his magnanimity,
already showcased at Harflur and to be seen again after
the battle of Agincourt, suddenly and inexplicably vanishes.
Astonishingly, at the height of the fray, it turns into a cold ruth-
lessness:

But hark, what new alarum is this same?
The French have reinforced their scattered men.
Then every soldier kill his prisoners!
Give the word through.

(4.6.35–7)[25]

The opportunity for Fluellen's response to this new turn of events is fully opened by the English captain Gower:

> they have burned and carried away all that was in the King's tent, wherefore the King most worthily hath caused every soldier to cut his prisoner's throat.

To which he adds, with appalling disingenuousness: 'O, 'tis a gallant king!' (4.7.8–10). With Fluellen's reply, the mask of 'good' or 'house' Welshman seems suddenly and decisively to slip as his Welsh 'accent' unexpectedly homes in on and ignites explosive material at the heart of some of the English words: 'Ay, he was porn at Monmouth, Captain Gower. What call you the town's name where Alexander the Pig was born?' (4.7.11–13) The moment is electrifying. It remains so however much we stiffen our sinews in an effort to secure the 'proper' reading, which the text quickly strains to re-establish. Here, briefly but significantly, the parody itself starts independently to signify. Once more, a name bursts the boundaries of straightforward reference.

Does Fluellen's Welsh accent effectively turn on those who have been laughing at it here? Does it unveil, in 'Alexander the Pig', a glimpse of a potential 'beastly transformation' dormant yet potent at the heart of the new Britain as corrosively as it was at the old? Does a sow-like Falstaff stalk even this field? Is the shining victory of Agincourt to be dimmed by the shadow of the atrocities at Bryn Glas? Fluellen presses home his comparison: Alexander killed his friend Clytus, just as 'Harry Monmouth' turned away Falstaff (4.7.44ff.). 'I'll tell you, there is good men porn at Monmouth' (4.7.51) he continues. As boys are now slaughtered, further throats cut (4.7.62), the ironies gather. Must 'big', or 'great' structures – Alexander the Great, or even Great Britain – inevitably harbour the same repressed beastliness of the sort that Welshness, breaching the boundaries even of the English language, seems always to announce? The Acts of Union had offered to make Wales and England one nation. Yet whatever Welsh misgivings might have been, a fear amongst the English must have whispered that such a Union could sap, dilute – nay, mutilate – their manhood. Perhaps, as Gower advises Pistol, Fluellen should be listened to: 'You thought because he could not speak English in the native garb he could not therefore handle an English cudgel. You'll find it otherwise...' (5.1.75ff.). We do. We will.

Onlie beget

To attempt to conquer and to pacify an alien culture by force of arms is one thing. To 'unify' one's own culture with a different one and to pronounce them equal in law in pursuit of the same end is quite another. The Acts of Union – the name, given in the nineteenth century, retains remorseless sexual implications – were always a somewhat forced conjunction and the anxiety that grows through the *Henry IV–V* cycle surely reflects that. For any proposal of 'equality' presupposes a likeness, beneath the trappings of language and way of life, whose establishment and maintenance is a vastly tricky project. In this case, its purpose dictates that Englishness, the whole cloth from which Britishness will be cut, be perceived as the defining feature of an unchanging 'human nature' and that it be presented as at least discernible and occasionally verifiable – however much that requires the triumph of faith over experience – in Wales and the Welsh.

Major obstacles to this perception must have been the battle of Bryn Glas and its aftermath, the emergence and rise of a triumphant Owain Glyn Dŵr and the fears of a barbaric Welsh expansion. Passing – like many Welsh events – quickly into the sphere of myth and legend, these became, by the time of Shakespeare's plays, the focus of an ideological contradiction whose complexities had – in the name of the new Britain – to be resolved. With the cementing of the Tudor claim to power, Welshness needed, at whatever cost, to be brought within the English pale, and the stresses and strains of the adjustments required by that programme are surely evident in these texts. As one Welsh Prince of Wales – Glyn Dŵr – sinks, another English one – Hal – dramatically rises to replace him. As, concomitantly, the threatening figure of a Llewellyn seems about to rise, so the wholesome caricature of a Fluellen brings it down to earth.

The volatile, unstable text that is Shakespeare's 'Britain'

shares a number of features with the text displayed in *Glas*. Examined historically, it is clear that the column called 'England' has always already been engaged with the column called 'Wales' across whatever borders may be proposed between them. There never was a static, unified and clearly defined England, absolutely distinct and separable from a static, unified and clearly defined Wales. And neither the English language nor the Welsh language has ever been uniformly current throughout each respective culture. All such texts, that is to say, as well as all the texts – in this case plays – that derive from and are addressed to them, covertly partake in the condition that *Glas* makes overt: fractured, dependent, jigsawed into place, their unified 'meaning' turns out to be generated more by our hopes, expectations and readings than by anything in their own material nature.

For many reasons, it has seemed appropriate in recent years to present the Irish dimension of the early modern 'Great Britain' project as its most revealing feature and to stress the unease with which the history plays engage it.[26] My purpose is certainly not to question the existence of this aspect of the plays, or its relevance for us in Britain, so much as to suggest a reordering of the priorities that have pushed it into prominence. For what must surely now be sensed, in our own post-devolution present, is that Welshness and its concerns throbs with a no less powerful, if occluded, pulse in the vasty deep of these plays. And periodically, its muffled beat invades and disrupts the step by which they march. After all, a modern post-devolution British audience cannot help but have its own thoughts about a Prince of Wales, and whenever they surface, the presentist project of making a material intervention into the past in the name of the present is effectively enabled.

Perhaps the greatest irony lies in the extent to which, since the nineteenth century, the unease about an integrated, non-devolved 'Britain' embodied in the plays has been suppressed in the name of a supposedly unified culture, which they have been systematically used to reinforce. The ideological processes that can in wartime present *Henry V* as a clarion call to British unity are undoubtedly complex ones. Yet the very idea of Great Britain as a single entity clearly depended upon, and was validated by, forces that now seem to have run their course. Their absence is bound to generate – as we more recently see –

nationalism of a different kind, currently identifiable with Irish-ness, Scottishness and Welshness. Continued difficulties may of course finally wake the most feared spectre of all: an English nationalism anxious once more to impose itself on those cul-tures with whom interaction is the price of self-identity.

The first response to that may well be the funereal tolling of Derrida's *Glas* (the word means knell) if not its bloody equival-ent, the appalling sound of blades being whetted on the stones of Bryn Glas. Meanwhile, the association of Wales with a feared, emasculating 'effeminacy' and the covert presence of that in the plays casts its own ironic shadow on a British colonial machine that, from the nineteenth century on, actively pro-moted Shakespeare in a context of institutionalised homosexu-ality in same-sex public schools, precisely because both the plays and that context were felt to be efficacious in the estab-lishment and reinforcement of the kind of 'manliness' appro-priate to Englishness and Empire.

Perhaps it would be misleading to offer this as an aspect of Housman's response to those 'blue remembered hills'. But it's worth acknowledging that it once again gives us occasion to applaud the perspicacity of two notoriously uncolonisable Irish critics. It was W.B. Yeats who proposed that, in effect, Shake-speare's history plays dramatised the clash between Celtic and Saxon views of the world, with the continuing battle between claimants for the crown a version of the momentous struggle for the British soul between an imaginative Celtic sensitivity on the one hand, and a calculating Saxon rationality on the other. This analysis led Yeats to admire the 'vessel of porcelain, Richard II', to despise 'the vessel of clay, Henry V', and ulti-mately, as Philip Edwards comments, to present Shakespeare as an honorary Celt.[27] No less pointedly, it was Oscar Wilde who suggested that the mysterious object of the Bard's private admi-ration might be none other than an irresistible boy actor 'of great beauty', born and bred in Wales. Unlike the demeaning confection 'Fluellen', his name, Wilde claims, was the entirely credible and wholly acceptable 'Willy Hughes'. It remains a thought of special piquancy that the most memorable of the unquiet spirits unleashed by the events at Bryn Glas might finally turn out to be 'Mr W.H.' And however unlikely, such a prospect would mean that a story that began with willies could also, at the very least, be said to end with one.

4
Aberdaugleddyf

What the heart knows

Consider three locations. First, a small tourist town on the
central coast of California. 'Enchanting and eccentric', it features a winsome cast of characters, whose daily concerns quickly
connect with our own. A major issue currently confronting them
is the relation of the town with the environment: the discovery of
off-shore oil fields has raised the possibility of invasion and disruption. At the story's centre stands the beautiful Miranda Jones;
'a shy environmental artist' who turns out, somewhat impercipi-
ently, to be 'dating a man who she does not know is an oil
magnate'. The potential conflict between the dictates of heart
and head here evidently and deliberately mirrors the more fundamental one between Nature (the sea, the unsullied coast) and
Culture (the industrial exploitation of oil) that invests the story
at large. Water and Oil, we learn, will never mix. But of course
failure to mix, inability to reconcile opposites, is the stuff of
which long-running soap operas – and this is one such – are
made. Perhaps this elemental truth stands as an example (to
quote the title of a specific episode) of What the Heart Knows.
Or is it all merely, as one critic puts it, 'for the most part stagey

trash of the lowest melodramatic order, in parts abominably written, throughout intellectually vulgar, and judged in point of thought by modern intellectual standards, vulgar, foolish, offensive, indecent, and exasperating beyond all tolerance'?

What the play says

Perhaps we should move quickly to the second location, where we can hope to encounter something rather more challenging. It is, after all, both ancient and British. Having just fought and won an exhausting battle against invading Roman legions, attacking precisely because of his refusal to pay tribute to the Empire they represent, a British king suddenly executes a surprising volte-face, inexplicably agrees to the payment he has so recently refused and abruptly proposes, as the play ends, a hastily cobbled-together alliance of dubious purpose and uncertain future:

> ...Let
> A Roman and a British ensign wave
> Friendly together: so through Lud's town march,
> And in the temple of great Jupiter
> Our peace we'll ratify, seal it with feasts.
> Set on there. Never was a war did cease,
> Ere bloody hands were washed, with such a peace.
> (5.4.480–6)

Coming right at the end of the play, this literally self-defeating moment seems to endorse contrariness of a rare order. As in the first case, there is no real mixing here. Indeed, an inability to achieve a persuasive reconciliation of opposites virtually undermines the story's credibility. Unsurprisingly, another critic, no less forceful, if slightly more polite than the first, finds 'much incongruity', even 'unresisting imbecility', in the piece. It's hard to imagine, on the face of it, that many would want to disagree with such a judgement.

Port in a storm

We can then move on to the third location, a material and concretely existing place that might be said almost to embody the commitment to disjunction and non-mixing evidenced by the first two. In fact, its name links them: 'Aberdaugleddyf'. 'Aberdaugleddyf' is, almost literally, a contradiction in terms. A Welsh place-name, it refers to two entities in the guise of one, or a point at which two separate things remain in unresolved suspension, so that they can be simultaneously glimpsed in a single word. For 'Aberdaugleddyf' nominates the mouth or confluence ('Aber') of two ('dau') streams, which jointly form the estuary of the Eastern and Western Cleddau rivers. And if that name seems – to English-speakers – characteristically illogical, and impenetrably, irritatingly Welsh, something of its indeterminate 'duality' seems oddly enough to transfer itself to the other name by which it is nowadays usually replaced. For that embodies a no less characteristic – and thus in the circumstances opposite – set of qualities that we should have to call English: the name is 'Milford Haven'.

Like many things English, the name 'Milford Haven' has a slightly dodgy air. After all, it's evident from other names in the area, 'Skomer', 'Skokholm', 'Grassholm', that marauding Norsemen onced used the 'haven' (i.e. harbour). So perhaps the apparently tranquil, placid, uncontradictory name 'Milford' derives, contradictorily, from that un-English warlike source?[1] However that may be, by now the name somehow suggests a kind of generic tranquility, which connotes and indeed confers its own sort of pastoral Englishness.[2] Just saying it is inexplicably comforting. But even in English a shadowy potential for contrariety persists. 'Milford Haven' is of course the name of the Welsh port central to Shakespeare's complex and demanding play *Cymbeline*, which is the second of the locations mentioned earlier. Yet it is also the name of the fictitious town – the first location – that supplies the title of the rather less demanding, if no less complex, American soap opera with which this chapter began. That too is called 'Milford Haven'. Anybody who considers both works would be forced to the conclusion that their respective heroines, Innogen in the case of Shakespeare, Miranda Jones in the case of the soap opera, constitute opposite, wholly unappeasable poles.[3] And yet the hint of a link remains, so that it's appropriate to point out that the critical strictures I presented as referring to the Californian 'Milford Haven' were in fact levelled, by their perpetrator George Bernard Shaw, at Shakespeare's play. The other set of condemnatory judgements – also levelled at *Cymbeline* – are those of Dr Johnson.[4]

My point is that the port's two names, 'Aberdaugleddyf' on the one hand, 'Milford Haven' on the other, stand as a sort of linguistic outcrop of its huge and unresolved cultural contrariness, itself a tribute to and symbol of an unceasing history of liminality. 'Milford Haven'/'Aberdaugleddyf' is a port. Like all ports, it is inescapably a place of eternally swivelling, contradictory modes: of ingress and egress, of in and out, of going and coming, of arrival and departure. That its names oscillate between the opposed poles of Welshness and Englishness, and Englishness and Californian Americanness – whilst somehow managing to caricature the essence of each – is simply an outward and manifest sign of an inward and unavoidable truth. Nothing is mixed or unified here. Nothing is finally resolved. Disjunction rules. Oil and water indeed.

Certainly water. For centuries, Milford Haven has actively functioned as a point of access to and departure from Britain, and like all ports has been involved with the kind of fundamental ebbing and flowing characteristic of a threshold or boundary. As such, it has for centuries served to focus the issues of foreignness and of domesticity underlying the concept of nationhood. Characteristically, it has also added its own contradictory inflection to that role. In the last decade of the eleventh century, the Normans invaded the area from mid-Wales. Since it remained Anglo-Norman in character, Milford Haven has been accurately described by J.F. Rees, its historian, as 'the vital artery of the Englishry' in that area.[5] Situated firmly within the borders of Wales, the port remained none the less true to its non-mixing disjunctive nature by contributing powerfully to the tensions that make that part of the Principality notoriously un-Welsh. To this day, its seat, the county of Pembrokeshire, enjoys the sobriquet (which is also an oxymoron) 'little England beyond Wales'.

Of course, Milford Haven's physical attributes present no essential contradiction. Its total navigable length of over twenty mile makes it, to quote a nineteenth-century topographer, 'one of the most extensive and secure harbours in the world', capable of 'receiving, at one time, 1000 ships of the line, and the same number of 50–gun ships, of frigates, of sloops of war and of transports...'[6] Well before that, it had enjoyed the status of chief port of embarkation for expeditions from Britain to Ireland. In 1649, Oliver Cromwell sailed from Milford Haven with his expeditionary force, landing in Dublin on 15 August to begin the ruthless and devastating campaign whose evils extend into the present day. Predictably, Shakespearean echoes abound. In September 1394 and May 1399, Richard II had sailed from Milford Haven to Waterford. On his return from the latter trip in July 1399, he landed at Milford Haven, shortly to surrender to Henry of Lancaster, who became Henry IV. The port also had potential as a major landing stage for the invasion of Britain. In August 1405, a French fleet with several thousand men sent by Charles VI of France disembarked there to join the rebellion of Owain Glyn Dŵr. And on 7 August 1485, a date close to many Elizabethan hearts, Henry, Earl of Richmond, landed at Milford Haven from France to begin the campaign that ended at Bosworth field and with his subsequent crowning as the Tudor monarch Henry VII.[7]

In Shakespeare's lifetime, the contradictory, liminal role of Milford Haven came most clearly to the fore in the light of the expected Spanish invasion. Almost literally, the place acquired the dimensions of *aporia* appropriate to the contradictions struggling within the history of its name. Peaceful, or warlike? On the one hand, a wonderful, natural haven and 'home' base, closely connected with the establishment of the Tudor dynasty. On the other, a site of potential foreign disruption and chaotic enemy subversion. In 1539, Thomas Cromwell had drawn attention to the need for fortification and two blockhouses were built. But the sailing of the Spanish Armada in 1588 raised a more urgent sense of alarm and drew on the fears earlier expressed about Milford's vulnerability. A Spanish landing there was certainly considered possible and although the Armada never arrived, Milford remained an obvious temptation for Spain. Queen Elizabeth ordered new fortifications to be built there in 1590. On 8 November 1595, a letter from the Bishop of St David's and the Justices of the County of Pembroke to Lord Burleigh, Lord High Treasurer of England, speaks at length of Milford Haven's strategic importance, its role as guarantor of national security, and the vulnerability it embodies. Its easy access to and from Ireland is of course stressed. Since the port also has, they say, 'a sufficient harbor-

ough for an infynite nomber of Ships' and is so well provided
for in terms of access to food and means of communication, its
capture by 'the Enemye' would necessarily prove disastrous.
The letter climaxes in a plea for Milford Haven to be fortified
and requests that an experienced engineer be sent to negotiate
the project.[8]

The resulting blockhouses were not a success, being judged
capable of disrupting friendly shipping as much as that of foes.
But somehow this botched effort serves to point up the
paradox that Milford Haven seems always to have embodied.
Both secure and vulnerable, a place of great domestic resource,
which also offers a tremendous advantage to an 'Enemye', the
port stands, perhaps more than anywhere in Britain, as a locus
of indeterminacy, a blank page on which a definition of the
nation might begin to be written.

In and out

There are few more powerful evocations of the sensations and
emotions irrevocably connected with the idea of departure and
arrival than those to be found in *Cymbeline*. Innogen's words are
only one example:

> I would have broke mine eye-strings, cracked them, but
> To look upon him till the diminution
> Of space had pointed him sharp as my needle;
> Nay, followed him till he had melted from
> The smallness of a gnat to air, and then
> Have turned mine eye and wept.
>
> (1.3.17–22)

The protracted and agonising shrinkings – literal and
metaphorical – involved in travel may be mitigated for us in an
age of supersonic flight, but here they display their ancient and
overpowering capacities to rend. In this play, centred as it is on
loss and restitution, on banishment and return, on exile and
homecoming, the figures of egress and ingress from and to a
'haven' pull, like tides, at a deep level. Their contradictory, elemental tugging can be felt everywhere in the play, from
Giacomo's slyly sexual, yet otherwise almost impenetrable,
paean to Innogen's virtue –

Sluttery, to such neat excellence opposed,
Should make desire vomit emptiness,
Not so allured to feed.

(1.6.44–6)

– to the curiously compelling ebb and flow of victory and
defeat between Romans and Britons, symbolically choreo-
graphed in dumb show in Act V, and then breathlessly
sketched in Posthumus's account, given in the play's characteristic mode in which logic and clarity bob helplessly along on
the surface, at the mercy of a deeper swell:

These three,
Three thousand confident, in act as many –
For three performers are the file when all
The rest do nothing – with this word 'Stand, stand',
Accommodated by the place, more charming
With their own nobleness, which could have turned
A distaff to a lance, gilded pale looks;
Part shame, part spirit renewed, that some, turned coward
But by example – O a sin in war,
Damned in the first beginners! – gan to look
The way that they did and to grin like lions
Upon the pikes o'th' hunters. Then began
A stop i'th'chaser; a retire; anon
A rout, confusion thick; forthwith they fly
Chickens the way which they stooped eagles: slaves,
The strides they victors made; and now our cowards,
Like fragments in hard voyages, became
The life o'th' need...

(5.3.28–45)

The play's notoriously compacted and contorted style, the con-
volutions of its plot, the indeterminacy of its components (who
is related to whom? which friend can be trusted? whose body
matches whose head?) generate a rhapsody of coming and
going, of passing and bypassing, of connection and disconnec-
tion. In fact, a continuing oscillation between coming in and
going out, ingestion and excretion, penetration and ejacula-
tion, seems both to chug away behind and to energise the confusions which, far from undermining the work, supply its

'signature'. In this context, Giacomo's intrusion into Innogen's bedroom becomes itself a tale of a British 'haven' infiltrated by scurrilous foreign forces. His secret incursion becomes an enemy 'voyage upon her' (1.4.152), its invasive metaphors speak of assaulting the 'walls' of Innogen's honour, the 'temple' of her mind (2.1.60–1).

Imperial preference

If the play's subterranean rhythms so evidently mimic those of ingress and egress, then it is appropriate that a port becomes its ultimate focus. Milford Haven is increasingly stressed as the plot unfolds and from the middle of Act 3 it dominates the whole play, locating its action firmly in Wales. In one sense, this serves to reinforce aspects of the developing 'island' role of Britain in history and, certainly, such a kingdom's status needs to be guaranteed by ports. Giacomo's Roman 'invasion' is paralleled by the more traditional action proposed by Lucius. But, confronting the latter's demands for tribute, Posthumus makes it clear that a difficult landing on the island will be the necessary cost of its exaction (2.4.15–20). Cloten's faith in Britain's inviolability strikes a similar chord, stressing, despite his oafishness, an insular integrity:

> Britain's a world
> By itself, and we will nothing pay
> For wearing our own noses.
>   (3.1.12–14)

The sense of Britain as a complete 'world' separate from the rest of Europe, that 'world the world without' to which Philip Edwards has drawn attention, obviously suits an island whose 'salt-water girdle', as Cloten terms it, both defines and protects its essential nature (3.1.78), as well as giving substance to the stance the Queen urges on Cymbeline:

> Remember, sir, my liege,
> The kings your ancestors, together with
> The natural bravery of your isle, which stands
> As Neptune's park, ribbed and paled in
> With oaks unscalable and roaring waters,

With sands, that will not bear your enemies' boats,
But suck them up to th' topmast.

(3.1.16–22)[9]

This expresses not only what G. Wilson Knight calls 'precisely the sentiments many Elizabethan Englishmen must have felt after the failure of the Spanish Armada'.[10] It also fosters an outward- as well as an inward-directed vision. The island, and in this case the port that symbolises its nature, offer themselves as nothing less than a seed-bed suitable for the growth of Empire.

Cymbeline is of course an important play amongst those that, as Philip Edwards puts it, 'reflected the growth and expansion of England as it began to develop into Great Britain and the British Empire.'[11] The role of 'havens' is of the greatest, defining importance in such a development. As the Queen continues to make clear, their denial to an invading enemy, however powerful, is vital:

A kind of conquest
Caesar made here, but made not here his brag
Of 'came and saw and overcame'. With shame –
The first that ever touched him – he was carried
From off our coast, twice beaten; and his shipping,
Poor ignorant baubles, on our terrible seas
Like eggshells moved upon their surges, cracked
As easily 'gainst our rocks.

(3.1.22–9)

Innogen may at one stage draw attention to a world outside British shores (3.4.138–9), indeed, she may insist that 'There's livers out of Britain' (141). But her central perception preserves an image of the island's separateness, a complete and finished 'world' within a world, that also captures something of the sense of 'haven':

I'th' world's volume
Our Britain seems as of it but not in't,
In a great pool a swan's nest ...

(3.4.138–40)

It's fitting and relevant, then, that the action quickly moves to what has earlier been termed 'blessèd Milford' (3.2.59), the

place that 'Wales was made so happy as / To inherit (3.2.60–1).
All roads appear to lead here, to the extent that 'Accessible is
none but Milford way' (3.2.82). Somewhat surprisingly, even
the Roman ambassador includes it in his itinerary, unaccount-
ably crossing the Severn on his way back to Rome, and moving
like 'Jove's bird, the Roman eagle' from 'the spongy south to
this part of the west' (4.2.348–50). The port acquires an almost
magical dimension, becoming a location where problems will
be resolved, disguises abandoned and discoveries made. In the
process, Wales as a whole takes on a somewhat surprising pastoral function, becoming the place for a 'quiet life' (3.3.30), a
world of 'caves' of 'rain and wind' (3.3.37–40) whose denizens
are benignly 'beastly: subtle as the fox for prey / Like warlike as
the wolf for what we eat': in short, the 'country' to a disturbed
and corrupted court. To an Innogen broadened (or made
patronising) by travel, the Welsh are certainly not the savages
of uninformed report:

> These are kind creatures. Gods what lies I have heard!
> Our courtiers say all's savage but at court;
> Experience, O thou disprov'st report!
>
> (4.2.32–4)

'Here in the west' (5.4.477) is where the alliance between
Rome and Britain will finally be forged (5.4.461). Here the
Roman eagle which began its long journey 'From south to west
on wing soaring aloft' (5.4.472) finally makes its historic land-
fall and turns into 'our princely eagle'. An updated *pax Romana*
clearly burgeons.

The idea is well rooted in British history. Emrys Jones has
pointed out that the play's Milford Haven setting readily acti-
vates the well-established association in the audience's mind
between the port and the landing of Richmond in 1485 and his
later accession as the first Tudor monarch. This is supported by
passages in Drayton's *Poly-Olbion* that speak of

> A branch sprung out of *Brute*, th'imperiall top shall get,
> Which grafted in the stock of great *Plantaginet*,
> The Stem shall strongly wax, as still the Trunk doth wither:
> That power which bare it thence, againe shall bring it
> thither

By *Tudor*, with faire windes from little Britain driven,
To whom the goodlie Bay of *Milford* shall be given;
As thy wise Prophets, *Wales*, fore-told his wisht arrive,
And how *Lewellins* Line in him should double thrive.

(5.49–56)

Later, precise reference is made to the two Cleddau rivers:

You goodlie sister Floods, how happy is your state!
Or should I more commend your features, or your Fate;
That *Milford*, which this Ile her greatest Port doth call
Before your equal Floods is lotted to your Fall!
Where was saile ever seene, or winde hath ever blowne,
Whence *Penbrooke* yet hath heard of Haven like her
owne?

(5.273–8)

It is of course important to the play that the Stuart successor to
the Welsh Tudors, James, is on the throne, continuing the Elizabethan settlements, for, as Jones argues, the precise symbolic
value of Britain's 'greatest port' resides in this connection.
James liked to style himself 'Jacobus Pacificus' and to present
himself as a ruler who embodied – literally – the peaceful
union of the nations making up the island of Britain. Far from
representing a break with the past, the Scottish king was seen as
emblematic of traditions that stretched back to Cymbeline's
time and beyond. He took pains to project an image at whose
centre there lay 'the fulfilment of the oldest prophecies of the
British people; it was a consummation rather than a violation of
England's oldest traditions'.[12]

James, whose motto was *Beati pacifici*, also loved to be called
the second Augustus (the Roman emperor during whose reign
Christ was born) and his subjects enjoyed seeing themselves as
'new Romans'.[13] He also liked to be thought of as the second
Arthur, emerging from the West to answer the call for ancient
British unity, and the second Brute, legendary founder of a
Britain that bore his name.[14] He referred to himself as a
'Western King', Ben Jonson termed him 'the Glory of our
Western World', and in Dekker's *Magnificent Entertainment*
(1603) he is addressed as

Great Monarch of the West, whose glorious Stem,
Doth now support a ripe Diadem,
Weying more than that of thy grandsire Brute . . .

It's unsurprising, given all this, that the idea of a western 'port'
or 'haven' informs the whole play.[15] Indeed Simon Forman's
brief, three-hundred-word eyewitness account of a performance
of *Cymbeline* mentions Milford Haven no less than three times.[16]
Appropriately, the play's oscillating rhythms make it the location for a departure that turns into a homecoming, or arrival.
And in the final scene of miraculous recognitions and resolu-
tions, it seems fitting that the terms are of alliance, of the
mixing and joining of interests. G. Wilson Knight's sense of the
play as a 'vast parable', one 'whose purpose is in part to empha-
sise the importance of ancient Rome in Britain's history', seems
confirmed by that.[17] Here, where a Celtic civilisation has given
way to an Anglo-Saxon one in a united Britain, Augustus's
Roman Empire is displaced westward: a putative British empire
merges with it, and will, it is implied, ultimately succeed it.[18]
Meanwhile, the Roman god Jupiter guides and protects both
(5.4.480–4).

Naturalising nature

Milford Haven, where Roman and British civilisations meet,
mix, and where the torch of empire passes from one to the
other, can thus, it seems, readily stand as an emblem of unity.
In June 1610, the year of *Cymbeline*'s composition, James's elder
son Henry was invested as Prince of Wales. Amongst the court
entertainments marking the occasion was Samuel Daniel's
masque *Tethys' Festival*, which explicitly refers to Milford Haven
in this capacity as

The happy port of union, which gave way
To that great hero Henry and his fleet,
To make the blest conjunction that begat
O greater and more glorious far than that.
(149–52)[19]

There's little doubt that, since 1945, British readings of the
play have responded to similar urgings and used them as a

basis for dealing with the play's complexities. However, the case – to which both Wilson Knight's and Emrys Jones's essays seem to assent – that Milford Haven can to this day properly be presented as a 'port of union' rests on an assumption that the early modern response to the play was uniform and that it would be permanently available and valid through to the present. But this leaves out of account a number of discordant rumblings detectable within the play's structure. Indeed, as we have seen in the cases of George Bernard Shaw and Dr Johnson, its discordancy is what most critics before 1945 commented on. For instance, at the play's heart, we can point to momentary but clear evidence of a British 'nationalist' sentiment that threatens to engulf the prevailing 'Roman' sense of unity and empire. Granted, this manifests itself largely in the mouths of villains – the Queen and the 'puttock' Cloten. None the less, Philip Edwards's reading, whereby 'Having won the battle [Britain] is free to abandon the nationalist intransigence which caused it, surrender the separatist claim and as an adult partner enter into a free union with Rome', seems rather more tempting than convincing.[20]

The problem lies in that notion of 'merging' and free union. For the play reveals, as much by its silences as by its manifest content, that the process is not without significant stresses and strains. After all, any future 'mixing' of Roman and British ways of life is surely implicitly to be modelled on and judged by the success or otherwise of the prior mixing of the cultures of Wales and England. This, evidently, is the point the Welsh setting seeks to affirm. And that raises a major difficulty in *Cymbeline*. Assertions of an achieved Britishness certainly abound. Posthumus is advertised boldly and approvingly as a 'Briton' (1.4.25; 5.3.74–5, 80), he is 'The Briton Reveller' (1.6.61) and a 'Briton peasant' (5.1.24). But where are the Welsh? Even though two-thirds of the play are set in Wales, we meet no native-born Welsh people there – unless we count the 'two beggars' of whom Innogen asks directions (3.6.8–9). Their status may be significant.

Indeed, Shakespeare's plays show a general decline in the number of Welsh characters and in the degree of their perceived Welshness, from the bilingual Owen Glendower and his Welsh-speaking daughter in *1 Henry IV*, to the garrulous but monolingual Fluellen, and the caricatured Sir Hugh Evans in

The Merry Wives of Windsor. Far from encountering and engaging with the Principality, what we meet by the time of *Cymbeline* is a blank space, a *Gwalia Deserta* whose citizenry are conspicuous by their absence and to whose culture the only concessions are Belarius's assumed name of Morgan/Mergan (3.3.106) and perhaps the name he awards to Arviragus, Cadwal. At first sight a traditional move from 'court' to 'country', from 'civil' life to the arms of nature, Innogen's sojourn in Wales may to some extent derive from pastoral convention (Simon Forman's reference to a setting involving 'the cave in the woods' reinforces the notion of a generalised pastoral location signalled by scenery). But it also has the dimensions of an excursion to the sort of bizarre nightmarish fairy-land characteristic of many folk-tales and it shares some of those disturbing features. A heroine, fleeing from a wicked stepmother, who finds sustenance and shelter in a cave with an odd 'family' of males, and who then apparently dies, only to be miraculously revived, has more in common with the story of Snow White than with the *Mabinogion.*[21] Innogen's response to the recognition by Cymbeline that his sons are alive in Wales, and that she has thus 'lost by this a kingdom' (5.4.374), finds her explicitly rejecting the notion that the family she discovers in Wales is the same as the one she inherits in England.

> No my lord,
> I have got two worlds by't.
> (5.4.374–5)

Perhaps the root of the matter lies there, in those 'two worlds'. The Welsh remained then, as they remain still, a distinct culture. Welsh people spoke, as a number of them still speak, a distinct tongue, and to some degree the names Milford Haven/Aberdaugleddyf record those differences meeting, but not mixing. We have seen that, as a port, Milford Haven's condition partakes less of unity than of *aporia*, contradiction, ambiguity, disjunction. The suspended duality that Welsh records and recognises in 'Aberdaugleddyf', English smoothes over, makes singular and 'naturalises' in 'Milford Haven'. In fact the issue of 'unity' cannot help but raise the question of what the series of Acts of Union between England and Wales finally involved.

Their avowed intention was overtly as admirable as it was simple: to unify the two cultures. Admittedly, the process would operate from the top down, regularising Wales's features in accordance with an English model, something that could only logically conclude by effectively causing the Principality to vanish. Thus Wales was 'shired'. The English system of 'counties' was imposed, as was English law. In removing what were, from an English viewpoint, 'divers rights usages laws and customs ... discrepant from the laws and customs of this realm', the goal was to make usual and acceptable what the very name of 'Welsh' insists is not so. As has been pointed out, the Old English *wælisc* means, abruptly, 'foreign'. In effect, the Acts of Union aimed to remove outlandish difference and to assert in its place native sameness; to domesticate, to 'naturalise', precisely in that word's sense both of establishing common consent concerning the natural order of things and of admitting to the rights of state citizenship.[22]

The language of the Acts is thus, revealingly, replete with notions of mixture and merging, expressing both the monarch's resolve that the 'said country or dominion of Wales shall be, stand and continue for ever from henceforth incorporated united and annexed to and with this his realm of England' and his aim 'utterly to extirp all and singular the sinister usages and customs' separating the two cultures. This, it is promised, will 'bring the said subjects of this his realm, and of his said dominion of Wales, to an amicable concord and unity'. However, since, regrettably, some of those subjects 'have and do daily use a speech nothing like, nor consonant to the natural mother tongue used within this realm', a major casualty of the process would be the Welsh language:

> all justices commisioners sherriffs coroners *escheators* stewards and their lieutenants and all other officers and ministers of the law, shall proclaim and keep the sessions courts hundreds leets, sherriffs courts and all other courts in the English tongue; and all oaths of officers juries and inquests, and all other affidavits verdicts and wagers of law, to be given and one in the English tongue; and also that from henceforth no person or persons that use the Welsh speech or language shall have or enjoy any manner office or fees within this realm of England, Wales, or other the

King's dominion, upon pain of forfeiting the same offices
or fees, unless he or they use and exercise the English
speech or language.[23]

The dilemma of all 'progressive' legislation is clearly evident
here. What to the initiating party seems elevating and equalising can readily swivel round so that to the incorporated party it
comes to seem demeaning, and depriving. Whatever else
happens, as an awkward, duplicitous 'Aberdaugleddyf' dwindles into a cohesive and self-identical 'Milford Haven', mixing
signally fails to take place. A Wales drained of Welshness
becomes part of the price at which Britishness is bought. If
twentieth-century Britain continues to wrestle with this
dilemma, *Cymbeline*, viewed as it must be from that perspective,
founders on it.

Living in the present

For what the play finally, helplessly hints at is the extent to
which the 'two worlds' that England and Wales comprise remain
two, not one. For all the agile opportunism of its ending, indeed
signalling as much by it, *Cymbeline* cannot resolve the contradiction that the notion of a British 'nation' embodies: a single,
unified and coherent entity perhaps, but one that is also
simultaneously multiple, and in the face of whose complexity
various, increasingly desperate programmes of 'naturalisation'
will always be urged. It is a process that extends well beyond
Shakespeare's day. Thus when, on 17 July 1917, the then British
Admiral of the Fleet was forced to change what was in the circumstances his somewhat embarrassing name from the German
'Battenberg' to the more reassuring English-sounding Mount-
batten, his 'naturalisation' immediately followed. And he was
instantly awarded the title of Marquis of Milford Haven.

If that twentieth-century detail tells us anything about *Cymbeline*, it does so as the by-product of the critical stance already
referred to: presentism. As has been said, presentist criticism's
involvement with the text is precisely in terms of those dimensions of the present that most clearly connect with the events of
the past. A fairly obvious area of potential presentist interest
lies in the recent development of so-called 'devolution' in
British politics as a means, not only of meeting the demands of

Scottish and Welsh national sentiment, but of helpfully connecting with aspects of the continuing situation in Ireland. It
was a great Irish poet, W.B. Yeats, who understood how fundamental such matters can be, writing 'One can only reach out to
the universe with a gloved hand – that glove is one's nation, the
only thing one knows even a little of.'[24] This principle is
reflected nowhere more intensely than in the massive re-negoti-
ation of power relationships between the four nations compris-
ing Britain that is currently at stake. Not for the first time in
history, but certainly for the first time concurrently and as
aspects of a planned development, separate parliaments or
assemblies now exist in Scotland, Wales and Northern Ireland.
There is also promised a 'Council Of The Isles' not, so far as
can be seen, dominated by England. So radical a series of political developments insists, surely, that the plays – some more
than others – of that glove-maker's son Shakespeare must be
read differently for the foreseeable future, and in accordance
with a revised scale of 'relevance'.

That the issues of national identity raised by devolution
should sponsor our readings of the second tetralogy of the
history plays is not, of course, an outlandish proposal. Nor is
the notion that these issues might also provide revealing access
to, say, *King Lear*, *Macbeth* and other works. Such readings will
prove of considerable interest, particularly in regard to what
they can tell us about the notion and development of an idea
of 'England' and 'Englishness' as well as about the construction
of the 'Great Britain' that to a considerable extent underlies
it.[25] However, and most significantly, the commitments to devolution made in 1997, and realised in 1999, also require that the
'Great Britain' project, chronicled and reinforced throughout
Shakespeare's plays, must henceforth be seen, not just as a
beginning, but as the inception of an enterprise that has now,
after four hundred years, reached its conclusion.

All ends, when they arrive, shape the beginnings that
precede them. The rereadings they unavoidably bring about
cannot help but generate intricate realignments of the texts at
stake. This means, as was pointed out above, that both tetralo-
gies of the history plays can never be read after 1999 in quite
the same way that they could be read before that date. The
same is obviously the case with *Cymbeline*. The triumphant
proposal that concludes its action seems initially to confirm

G. Wilson Knight's sense of the play as one in which the merger of a Celtic civilisation with an Anglo-Saxon one provides the basis of a united Britain destined eventually to achieve an empire in succession to its Roman forebears.[26] Cultural unity and imperial destiny thus stand as key elements of God's/Jupiter's ultimate plan for a limitless future world order for which the British Empire acts both as model and guarantor.

So far as Wilson Knight was concerned, confirmation of God's good sense in this matter remained in evidence well into the latter years of the twentieth century. Writing in support of the Falklands war in 1982, he makes his position, and its Shakespearean roots, chillingly clear: 'I have for long accepted the validity of our country's historic contribution, seeing the British Empire as a precursor, or prototype, of world-order. I have relied always on the Shakespearean vision ... '.[27] However, a presentist analysis will require a decisive refocusing on and rereading of the same events in *Cymbeline* for, to put the matter simply, the constitutional developments established in 1999 must alter the status of the ultimate ecstatic vision with which the play concludes and, by loading it with ironies, charging it with pathos, or stripping away its pretensions, must change irrevocably both what it 'says' and what we are able to say about it. In short, the loom on which a consensus of post-1945 readings of the play was woven is precisely the instrument that, reexamined post-1999, must undo them. Thus, what *Cymbeline* presents as the beginning of a divine and transcendental world strategy cannot help but dwindle, after 1999, to the status of a material time-bound human project whose end is now clearly in view.[28]

It also brings its own, deepening ironies and these cannot help but invest and now perhaps determine our reading of the play. All societies try to 'naturalise', to harmonise, to create unity in the name of nationhood. Perhaps imperialism simply brings this to the fore, and perhaps what we experience as cultural imperialism represents an extension internationally of the same homogenising process. Ironically, one of the main agencies producing the barren, emptied Welsh culture mentioned above may be the active promotion, through and on behalf of a militant English-speaking world order, of the plays of Shakespeare. *Cymbeline* may turn out itself to be the ailment that the play helps us to diagnose. If so, it will thus simply, if

inadvertently, reveal the genuine cost of a Bard whose trappings of spurious universalism are the least attractive of his
modern accoutrements.

Currently, the United States proclaims and firmly prosecutes
the 'equalising' principle announced in its motto *E Pluribus
Unum* with the same rigour that Henry VIII pursued the Acts of
Union between England and Wales. But if history tells us anything, it tells us that the 'naturalising' process, even when it
involves the mixing of culture with nature, and especially when
it involves the mixing of cultures themselves, has a potential for
pathos that requires constant vigilance. As we have already
noticed, and as The Heart Knows, even in the idyllic cultural
setting of Milford Haven, California, the principle of *E Pluribus
Unum* does not guarantee that oil will mix with water. If the
Shakespearean echoes seem here to be muddled by the choice
of Christian names such as Miranda, with their echoes of
similar encounters where innocent nature and a corrupting
culture may seem to meet, we can find other, perhaps more
brutal, examples that cast their shadow on the concluding
vision of *Cymbeline*. Certainly in our time, Milford Haven can
hardly claim to have been a model for the process of mixing, or
naturalisation.

By the twentieth century, the physical attributes of the
harbour had made it one of the major oil-importing ports in
Europe. However, in February 1996 a particular tragedy struck.
A gigantic oil tanker ran aground whilst trying to enter the
port. Its name, *Sea Empress*, carries its own ironic echoes both of
the Haven's history and of the imperial destiny prophesied in
Cymbeline, to say nothing of the events foretold in the Californian soap opera. Less ironic is the fact that, as a result of the
accident, the tanker discharged approximately 72,000 tonnes
of crude oil into the sea around the Welsh coastline, devastating its abundant wildlife and polluting its beautiful beaches
with a severity that made and makes it an oil-and-water cata-
strophe unique in European history.

Those who visit Milford Haven today may register a final, not
entirely serious irony. In 1793, long before the *Sea Empress* disaster, a group of Quaker families from Nantucket Island, Mass-
achusetts, moved to live in Britain; specifically, to Milford
Haven. Amongst them were a young man called Timothy and
his wife Abiel. Timothy died at Milford Haven in 1814. His

tombstone in the Quaker graveyard there reveals that his surname was Folger. One of his most illustrious descendants (through Peter Folger (1617–90) also of Nantucket) was Henry Clay Folger (1857–1930), founder of the famous Folger Shakespeare Library in Washington, DC.[29] And the company for which Henry Clay Folger worked for almost fifty years, eventually becoming its president and acquiring the fortune that made the Folger Shakespeare Library possible, was, with an irony worthy of the Bard himself, none other than Standard Oil.

5

The Old Bill

Law and order

Berlin, 1945. It seems distinctly odd that, in the late summer of
that year, at the end of the most destructive war in human
history, the victorious allied armies occupying the German
capital should take it upon themselves to act as Masters of the
Revels. Yet in addition to the countless tasks inseparable from
the administration of a huge city now reduced to rubble, each
of them solemnly embarked on the business of censoring plays.

In the American sector, the Office of Military Government
of the United States (OMGUS) duly appointed a number of so-
called Theatre Officers. It also circulated two lists: a 'black' list
of proscribed plays, and a 'white' list of works whose public
performance was deemed to be of benefit to a defeated, trau-
matised populace in need of radical political re-education. The
black list featured two major pieces by Shakespeare: *Julius
Caesar* and *Coriolanus*. Performances of these were roundly
banned, in the light of their supposed 'glorifications of dicta-
torship'. The white list contained *Macbeth* and *Hamlet*, the
former held brusquely to affirm that 'Crime Does Not Pay', the
latter's inclusion more curiously justified on the basis of its
alleged treatment of 'corruption and justice'.[1]

More than fifty years on, in London on 19 October 1999, the state visit to Britain of President Jiang Zemin of China was marked by a series of scuffles between some of the spectators and the police. Protesters against China's record on human rights shouted slogans and tried to unfurl appropriate banners. Their efforts were vigorously suppressed, apparently in sympathy with the Chinese President's frequently expressed sensitivities in the matter. His view that, in a civilised society, dissident voices should be kept firmly in check was evidently fully supported by the British government. That afternoon it was arranged that he should visit the new Globe Theatre in Southwark. Plainly, the issue wasn't whether the President liked Shakespeare's plays or not. His visit raised the much more complex question of cultural meanings in modern Britain and the social and political use to which both plays and Bard may be put in generating them. The incidents in this case point to the operation of a well-defined binary structure: dissidence and disruption on the one hand (located in the protesters) and appeasement and pacification on the other (located in Southwark).

It seems not unreasonable to suggest that these events in the middle and towards the end of the twentieth century hint at – even coyly propose – a certain meaningful role for Shakespeare in the general scheme of things British and American. Effectively, they construct him as an agency of law and order.[2]

On watch

Of course the notion of William Shakespeare as 'The Old Bill', a Bard deployed as an instrument of 'policing', is scarcely a new development.[3] *Hamlet* in particular seems to have been associated with that sort of activity almost from the first. Two of its earliest recorded performances took place, remarkably enough, on board a ship off the coast of Sierra Leone. The journal of William Keeling, captain of the East India Company's vessel *Dragon*, bound with the *Hector* and the *Consent* for the East Indies, gives the details:

> 1607, Sept. 5. I sent the interpreter, according to his desier, abord the Hector whear he brooke fast, and after came abord mee, wher we gaue the tragedie of Hamlett.

The performance's 'policing' purpose becomes clear in a later
entry;

> 1608, Mar. 31. I envited Captain Hawkins to a ffishe
> dinner, and had Hamlet acted abord me: which I permitt
> to keepe my people from idleness and unlawful games, or
> sleepe.[4]

In truth, the notion of the Bard as a kind of policeman lies at a
deep and sensitive level in the English-speaking psyche. The
legitimate theatre's long, Shakespeare-fuelled climb to its
present summit of respectability has always required the conspicuous shedding of various degrees of inherited 'lawlessness',
followed by the acquisition, among audiences at least, of the
lineaments of probity and solid citizenship. Avenues, roads and
streets named after the playwright have, since the nineteenth
century, threaded decorous paths throughout British suburbia.
His likeness underwrites banknotes and credit cards. In
Chicago, the fourteenth police district has long been known as
'Shakespeare'.

Congruent tendencies among veteran Shakespearean scholars are not unknown. W.W. Greg, hero of the 'new biblio-
graphy', virtual founder of modern Shakespearean textual
scholarship and author of the magisterial, law-and-order
enforcing *The Editorial Problem in Shakespeare* (1942), bonded
eagerly with the constabulary, recording that, during the First
World War, he drove a police car 'for Scotland Yard'. Later in
life, the same rectitudinous zeal impelled him to 'enrol as a
special constable and to drive a car once more for Scotland
Yard during the general strike of May 1926'.[5] Unsurprisingly,
Greg also enjoyed detective novels. His favorite was Michael
Innes's classic, *Hamlet, Revenge!* (1937), in which a murder
mystery is solved by a detective in the context of a modern
performance of the play.[6] The novel notably draws attention to,
and to a small extent focuses on, some of the moments when
the play *Hamlet*, rather than any of its characters, seems to take
on a 'supervisory' role in respect of its audience, reaching out
into it in order to direct, regulate or 'police' its responses.

Fell sergeant

As Innes need not point out, one of the most effective examples occurs right at the beginning of the play. A man comes out onto the stage, dressed as a soldier and carrying the large military spear, the partisan. He takes up a position, evidently as a sentry. A second man enters, similarly dressed, also carrying a partisan. He approaches the first man, in the role of a relieving sentry. Suddenly, he freezes, manifests extreme fear, and brings his spear from the 'rest' or 'trail' position into an offensive one. The effect is startling. It immediately involves the audience in an atmosphere of grotesque unease, which, they can see, already generates breaches of military discipline on stage, forcing these soldiers into error. Indeed, discipline so completely deserts the second man (it is Barnardo) that he blurts out the play's first line, not as a soldier, but merely as a very frightened onlooker: 'Who's there?'. In consequence, the play's second line, uttered by the first man (Francisco), manifests all the exasperation of the professional who, having kept his nerve, seeks to correct his colleague on matters of military procedure: 'Nay, answer me. Stand and unfold yourself.' Barnardo, the challenger challenged, then nervously confirms the restoration of order by uttering the password 'Long live the King.'

The irony is intense. The King, we suspect, will not live long. We know that his predecessor did not. Worse, a hint of the presence of that predecessor's ghost is the factor that ignites the sentry's nervousness, and provokes his indiscipline. But it is in that simple movement of a spear, from an inoffensive to an offensive position, that the play, as it were, first speaks. Before one of its characters utters a word, that silent gesture reaches out into the auditorium, to coerce, marshal and decisively direct the emotional traffic. Of course, all art engages in this sort of thing. All plays have designs on their audiences that they promote through the wide variety of means the medium places at their disposal. But *Hamlet* seems remarkable for the degree to which it seeks to monitor, moderate or 'police' responses to itself and, ultimately, for the self-consciousness with which it draws attention to its own activities in this sphere. 'Look,' it periodically seems almost to boast, 'see how I can control you'.

Making a statement

I refer deliberately to the *play*'s activity in this regard, not to
that of any of its characters, although they too, as we have seen,
will be individually involved. Indeed, it is almost a common-
place that most of them engage in some sort of policing or
supervising activity. The Ghost watches and comments on
Hamlet's remonstration with his mother; Polonius notoriously
arranges the surveillance of Laertes, and of Hamlet and
Ophelia, and in fact meets his death while spying. In truth,
Hamlet himself seems to act very much as a kind of policeman
in his own play. He constantly tries to steer our responses, to
tell us what to think, how to assess the events we encounter. His
soliloquies are nothing if not a series of urgent recapitulations,
siftings of evidence and 'supervising' interventions into the
tumultuous action. Like other 'great ones', rarely 'unwatched'
in Claudius's court, the Prince 'polices' Ophelia's funeral, and,
most famously, uses a performance of *The Mousetrap* to place
Claudius under observation and secure evidence against him.
It's hardly surprising that the cumulative effect of all these individual efforts at moulding, shaping or recording the behaviour
of others is to confirm *Hamlet* as a play of monitoring, watching, eavesdropping and trap-setting. That the Prince should
finally picture his own condition as one of penal confinement,
'Denmark's a prison' (2.2.243), and present his own demise in
terms of resolute police action '...as this fell sergeant
Death / Is strict in his arrest' (5.2.341–2) comes as no surprise.

 Less overt moments of policing are not hard to find. One of
the most startling occurs in Polonius's interchange with his spy
Reynaldo:

Polonius: Marry, sir, here's my drift
 [...]
 Your party in converse, him you would sound,
 Having ever seen in the prenominate crimes
 The youth you breathe of guilty, be assur'd
 He closes with you in this consequence:
 'Good sir', or so, or 'friend', or 'gentleman',
 According to the phrase or the addition
 Of man and country.
Reynaldo: Very good, my lord.

Polonius: And then sir, does a this – a does – what was I about
   to say? By the mass, I was about to say something. Where did
   I leave?
Reynaldo: At 'closes in the consequence'.
Polonius: At 'closes in the consequence', ay, marry.
   He closes thus: 'I know the gentleman . . .

                                                   (2.1.38–55)

The introduction into any play of a moment when an actor
appears to forget his or her lines is a high-risk strategy. It risks
unravelling the very fabric of the art. It courts that disaster in
the hope of gaining advantage, using 'error' to pursue a more
subtle accuracy and, by its sly turning of the nuts and bolts of
the play into a statement that the play itself suddenly makes,
engages in a manipulative 'policing' of considerable subtlety.[7]

   Polonius's concern here, after all, is with spying: with the
ways in which concrete information yields itself to the resourceful probing of a secret agent who may 'By indirections find
directions out.' When he seems to forget his lines, the serpentine plotter of the play's world turns abruptly into a mere performer caught short in ours. As Polonius collapses into the actor
who is playing him, his tawdry guff about truth crumbles in the
face of a contesting 'reality', which bursts out from the stage to
land explosively in the middle of the audience. The actor who
momentarily and apparently disastrously peeps out from behind
the figure of Polonius calls that figure's entire project into question by indicating to us that this is a play: that he who has been
talking of investigative pretence, of carefully misleading suggestion, of acting a part, is himself, here and now, acting.

   The impact on the audience must be considerable. It's as if,
at a stroke, we found ourselves unceremoniously pitched back-
stage, into the play's material, quotidian innards. A dizzying
epistemological gulf suddenly yawns. Who is speaking here,
actor or 'character'? Where is reality located, on or off the
stage? In that sudden, explosive confusion, before its hasty res-
olution by Reynaldo, the audience feels itself firmly nudged in
the direction of one of *Hamlet*'s central concerns. It's a calculated moment of jolting realignment. Those who entered the
theatre as spectators suddenly find themselves stumbling, as
participants, in a no man's land whose indistinct and tangled
paths lead inexorably to *The Mousetrap*.

Hostile witness

Of course, *Hamlet* is well known in any case for its exposition of the notion that plays are able to manipulate their audiences rather more directly: that they have a forensic 'policing' potential that can even provoke spontaneous confession. The Prince's claim that a powerfully delivered speech can 'make mad the guilty and appal the free' (2.2.558) does not lack confidence, and his assurance –

> I have heard
> That guilty creatures sitting at a play
> Have, by the very cunning of the scene,
> Been struck so to the soul that presently
> They have proclaim'd their malefactions.
> For murder, though it have no tongue, will speak
> With most miraculous organ.
>
> (2.2.584–90)

– reflects a playwright's self-interest in connecting the performance of *The Mousetrap* with a long and substantial anecdotal tradition confirming the link between 'playing' and the actual social world. The understanding that the one carries imperatives for the other is reinforced by the suggestion that plays harbour a summary, prosecuting power enabling them somehow to reach out and make a kind of juridical contact with their audiences' private lives and individual consciences.[8]

But the flurry of play- and stage-references preceding *The Mousetrap* scarcely prepares us for the breathtaking audacity of what happens during its performance, although it does serve, by its references to playing companies, the theatre-war, and even by the player's graphic presentation of Pyrrhus as a Hamlet-like revenger, frozen on the brink of action, to construct an appropriate context. Thus Hamlet's account of a once-seen 'excellent play, well digested in the scenes, set down with as much modesty as cunning' (2.2.435ff.), his comments on the 'purpose of playing', his advice to the actors, his remarks on dumb-shows and on Polonius's acting can be seen as part of a deliberate strategy. When actors talk, in a play, about the mechanics of theatre and of acting, the effect must be to intensify an audience's awareness of its own presence and

function. Polonius's ready assumption of the applauding spectator's role in respect of Hamlet's rendition of lines from a
play, 'Fore God, my lord, well spoken, with good accent and
good discretion' (2.2.462–3), offers a coercive model.

The climax then comes when the issue of audience-response
moves to the centre of the stage. Claudius's blankness in the
face of the plain depiction of his crime in the dumbshow that
precedes *The Mousetrap* has of course famously exercised critics
over the years. How is it that he remains apparently unmoved?
Does his silence indicate superb self-control, which breaks
down only when the performance proper begins? Does it
suggest that the murder of his brother did not in fact follow the
sequence or use the method described by the Ghost? Does it
therefore mean that the Ghost is unreliable? Does Claudius in
fact fail to notice the dumbshow? Does he watch it but, because
of its formal elaboration, fail to notice that it applies to him?
No doubt there are a number of other possible explanations.[9]

It's an interesting reflection of modern presuppositions concerning art, and especially drama, that this matter should be
thought to constitute a 'critical problem' or even a playwright's
error. For it now seems reasonable to argue, to the contrary,
that Claudius's null response represents another of those
moments when the play, rather than one of its characters,
speaks. Having primed its audience to raise its own awareness
of itself, having led it to expect that audiences should and will
respond in a specific mode, that guilty creatures sitting at a play
will proclaim their malefactions, it suddenly and sensationally
presents us with a very important member of an audience who
does none of these things.

Claudius's failure to respond to the dumb-show is not
an 'error' or a 'mistake' made by Shakespeare. It's not something that goes 'wrong'. Or, rather, like Polonius's forgetting of
his lines, it's the sort of 'wrongness' that, once confronted,
begins to reveal what our inherited notions of 'rightness'
conceal from us. In effect, directed as it is at the audience of
Hamlet as much as at the 'inner' audience of the Prince and
Horatio, it represents – once more, as right at the play's beginning, by movements made in silence – a breathtaking defeat of
expectations that have been carefully and stealthily aroused
and unthinkingly embraced. Any confusion or dismay it generates – soon dispelled by subsequent events – not only mimics in

us the roller-coaster of emotions depicted on stage by the Prince. It also deepens and sophisticates our perception of both Hamlet and Claudius. In the event, *The Mousetrap* doesn't work very effectively and Hamlet's assertion to the contrary hints at both perversity and desperation. Indeed, the fact that Claudius remains largely impervious to the cardboard accusations of a Player King and Queen operates to his distinct advantage. Suddenly, Hamlet's opponent seems stronger, subtler, more sophisticated. He begins to intrigue, bewilder and perhaps ever so slightly to charm us as much as he disturbs and repels.

In short, *The Mousetrap* sets in motion a new and intricate see-saw. For if *Hamlet* shows us anything at this point, it shows us a highly complex villain whose corruption demands to be viewed in the light of, if not to be mitigated by, the pitiable human situation it generates: that of a man torn by the conflicting demands of criminal passion and remorse, and held to the flames by an obduracy that is also self-control. In addition, and by the same token, it presents us with a no less complex and increasingly reckless protagonist who, in the name of 'justice', will impulsively commit violent murder before our eyes: the same crime that he is dedicated to revenge. Hamlet's role as both killer and avenger, an identity clearly symbolised by the figure of Pyrrhus, cannot but complicate the play. In the view of Harold Jenkins, it ranks as a factor 'of the most profound significance, without a grasp of which the play cannot be understood'.[10] In the end, far from simply representing corruption on the one hand and justice on the other, Claudius and Hamlet seem, as 'mighty opposites', to be not unequally matched. When, in the final moments of the action, with bodies strewn about the stage, Fortinbras orders

> Let four captains
> Bear Hamlet like a soldier to the stage,
> For he was likely, had he been put on,
> To have prov'd most royal; and for his passage,
> The soldier's music and the rite of war
> Speak loudly for him.
> Take up the bodies...
>
> (5.2.400–6)

– it's tempting to propose that if 'he' in line 402 refers to Hamlet, then 'his' in line 403 refers to Claudius.

Royce's choices

If *Hamlet*'s 'policing' interventions serve ultimately to cloud the differences between hero and villain, they do so as part of a broader function that not only muddies the distinction between play-world and real world, but disturbingly reduces the distance between right and wrong. In the end, this hugely complicates the play, making its dilemmas to some extent unresolvable, and perhaps constituting the basis of the enigma from which its capacity to arrest and disturb derives.

If we now return to Berlin in 1945, it thus seems proper to ask on what basis a play as fundamentally complex as this could have recommended itself to the United States military authorities as an exemplary moral and political instrument, especially in terms as apparently straightforward as its treatment of 'corruption and justice'. It's a particular and instructive instance, perhaps, of a larger, well-attested tendency whereby a peculiar intimacy has often been felt to pertain between Shakespeare's world and the oncoming modern one. It hints, seductively, that we constitute a uniquely sympathetic audience for his plays. Indeed, a case can be made that the familiar – and evidently absurd – impression that Shakespeare somehow wrote his plays specifically 'for' us may rest on something more than fantasy. It doesn't imply – except metaphorically – that a post-war society could reasonably claim to be the audience at which the plays were actually aimed. But it does suggest that our sense of being present at the end of processes whose beginnings they signal might generate a particularly intense and hitherto unavailable feeling of recognition. For what confronts us in the plays, such a view suggests, is not the set of permanent, history-transcending truths of whose presence some critics have managed to convince themselves. It is more the outline – dimly perceived, yet now increasingly discernible – of a matching ideological relationship. A group of twenty-first-century theatre-goers might, after all, legitimately claim to share something unique with the plays' first audiences. That is, nothing less than a close encounter with 'modernity'; they at its beginning, we at its end; they from the point of view of the 'early' modern, we from that of the 'post'.[11]

The Shakespearean judgements made in Berlin in 1945 seemed to observers at the time to be quintessentially 'American'. They were also quintessentially 'presentist', as that term has been defined above, whereby material aspects of the present determine the agenda for a crucial engagement with the past. There was good reason for both. Prior to the Hitler period, German culture had been the envy of the Western world and a very high proportion of that world's major philosophers, scientists and theologians had worked and written in the German language. By contrast, the English-speaking culture of the United States was not particularly highly regarded – certainly not by Nazified Germans, who might prefer it to Russian culture, but undoubtedly considered it inferior to their own. Yet a major shift in cultural relationships was obviously now on the cards. The baton of leadership in the English-speaking world had passed from Britain to the United States. And if United States culture was to become a dominant world force in the years after 1945, one of its first acts in pursuit of that goal would have to be the imposition, in Berlin, of its lineaments, and the eradication of those that preceded them.

To exaggerate only slightly, the proposal that *Hamlet* was at this juncture preferable to *Coriolanus* heralds nothing less than a new world order. In it, the United States, not Britain, effectively speaks for a triumphant and belligerent Anglo-Saxon order, taking upon itself the responsibility of making a portentous assessment of the writings of its most prestigious author. Indeed, the portentousness is underlined by the fact that the judgement precisely reverses one made by an earlier, no less prestigious, but distinctly 'Englished', American voice – that of T.S. Eliot who had notoriously pronounced *Hamlet* an 'artistic failure' and cited *Coriolanus* as 'Shakespeare's most assured artistic success'.[12] In other words, what confronts us here is a 'presentist' reading of *Hamlet*, made in and for the new 'present', which began in 1945, and whose shape remains still just about discernible at the beginning of the twenty-first century. As the tip of a huge cultural and political iceberg, it offers a brief but revealing hint of some of the immense, if submerged, political, social and historical structures that sustain it. The sources of such a reading cannot fail to be of great interest. They lie in the career of Mauriz Leon Reiss.

He was a professional actor. Born on 30 March 1891, in Dolina, Galicia (latterly Poland), Reiss was employed in the German-speaking theatre and, changing his name to Leo Reuss, enjoyed a successful career in Vienna, Hamburg and Berlin, where he worked for a number of years with the likes of Erwin Piscator, Leopold Jessner and Bertolt Brecht.[13] However, by 1935, the restrictive race-laws of the Nazi regime had virtually deprived Reuss of his livelihood. As a Jew, it became impossible for him to find work in Germany, and he retreated to Austria. There, *in extremis*, he hit upon an audacious strategy. Carefully acquiring a number of intently observed verbal and physical mannerisms, he manufactured and then took on a wholly new identity: that of a Tyrolean mountain peasant, rude, self-taught, but endowed with a range of 'natural' acting talents, whose name was 'Kaspar Brandhofer'. Cloaked in this alter ego's rustic charm and protected by his Christianity, Reuss impressed men of the theatre as influential as Max Reinhardt and Ernst Lothar to the extent that 'Kaspar Brandhofer' was given the important part of Herr von Dorsday in a dramatisation of Arthur Schnitzler's story *Fräulein Else*.

The play's opening in Vienna proved memorable. 'Kaspar Brandhofer' was hailed as a potential star and the *Reichspost* called him the 'sensation of the evening'. A glittering future seemed to beckon. None the less, returning home after the first night, Reuss reported that he felt, not triumph, but emptiness and loneliness. Everyone was interested in 'Kaspar Brandhofer', he claimed, but 'niemand fragte nach mir, nach Leo Reuss'. His creation threatened to become a monster (he uses the word *Golem*), which, colluding with the eradication of Leo Reuss, seemed to demonstrate that the Nazi race-laws remained more powerful than the trick he had devised to defeat them. Shortly afterwards he and his wife emigrated to the United States, where he sought work as an actor in Hollywood. For this purpose he changed his name once more. As 'Lionel Royce' he managed, before his death in April 1946, to secure a succession of small parts in a number of films ranging in quality from *Confessions of a Nazi Spy* (1939) and *Charlie Chan in Panama* (1944), to *Gilda* (1946). Inevitably, in most of these, he played the part of an unsavoury 'German'; usually a Nazi.

No doubt the ironies of Royce's life-story stir numerous echoes in the experience of many citizens of Europe and the

United States during the 1930s and 1940s. His are remarkable only because the stratagem involved in the 'Kaspar Brandhofer' episode brings to the fore particular aspects of an actor's situation. At its centre lies the notion of some concrete, unified core, some indivisible, coherent 'real self' from which acted parts are projected: the 'me' that, in Royce's case, lies behind the 'Brandhofer' he acts, as well as behind the part that 'Brandhofer' acts. Obviously it would be of no help to him to point out that 'Brandhofer's' success is itself a triumph of acting, or that the 'real' Reuss is almost as much a confection as 'Brandhofer' when set against an original 'Reiss'. The phonetic and orthographic journey Reiss–Reuss–Royce marks an odyssey of part-playing, its cruellest irony unveiled in its final development, where 'Royce's' acting turns him into the image of his own fundamental enemy, the villainous Nazi.

In Royce's particular case, however, the irony is peculiarly reinforced by the cunning of the Schnitzler story which fuels the success that finally undermines him, destroying his identity, necessitating the move to Hollywood and forcing the ultimate traumatic transformation from Reuss to Royce. *Fräulein Else* concerns a neurotic young woman who, while staying at a fashionable spa hotel, receives a letter from her mother to say that her father is disastrously in debt. The only way out of this situation is to procure an immediate loan, and her mother urgently requests that Else asks a friend of her father's, Herr von Dorsday, who is staying at the hotel, to come to the rescue. Von Dorsday agrees, but on one condition: that Else permits him to view her naked for fifteen minutes. Considering the proposition, the highly-strung Else becomes more and more hysterical, and finally adopts the sensational stratagem of appearing publicly naked in the hotel's music room, in front of all the hotel guests, including Dorsday. She then collapses, feigns unconsciousness, and finally kills herself by taking an overdose of veronal.

It's a disturbing, intensely erotic tale of the sensual and financial impulses lying beneath the veneer of twentieth-century civilisation and it certainly casts a number of brilliantly sardonic reflections on the theme of women's relationship to men. Schnitzler's wry pre-Freudian insights abound. The notion that 'everything in this world has its price' has broad implication, and leads ultimately to Else's bitter comment on her parents, to the effect that 'they've brought me up to sell myself in one way or another' (Schnitzler 50, 64, 65). It's also evidently a story of the primal challenge involved in human nakedness, of an animal and fiscal final reality, initially cloaked by social convention, but then brutally exposed by the same society's irresistible economic and sexual imperatives. The manipulative character of von Dorsday contributes powerfully to this complexity and of course is of obvious interest to the story of Reuss/Royce.

Von Dorsday is an art dealer from Vienna, a 'social climber' whose insistence on an unacceptable bargain involving money and human flesh might well (to take up but one of its Shakespearean echoes) begin to imply, in Schnitzler's world, the veiled possibility of his Jewishness. This irony clearly adds its own dimension to Reuss's assumption, as a Jew, of the Christian disguise of 'Brandhofer' in order to act the part. As a Jewish citizen of Vienna, Schnitzler's sensitivities in the matter are often subtly in play throughout his work and Else's Molly-Bloom-like and increasingly feverish musings make a point of the suggestion that, like 'Brandhofer', von Dorsday may not be as Christian as he appears: 'What good does your first-class tailor do you, Herr von Dorsday? Dorsday! I'm sure your name used to be something else...' and, later, 'What's the man's name? Herr von Dorsday. Funny name...'[14] The reverberations of that for his impersonator are evident. The story's prevailing sense of theatricality, its reiterated emphasis on role-playing, is further reinforced by Else's repeated references to the forthcoming unveiling of her own 'real', finally naked, self as 'the performance, the great performance'. The connection with Reuss's own 'real' position gives this a disturbing dimension. Else's dismissal of Dorsday, 'He talks like a bad actor', adds a particularly ironic dimension to the 'sensation of the evening' (Schnitzler 51).

Seen in the light of our subsequent experience, such ironies probe to a deeper, even more uncomfortable, level. We know that in totalitarian societies, drama often functions as a preferred vehicle for criticism, protest, or the assertion of an alternative but officially impermissible world-view of how things really are.[15] A play's nature as a 'public' art form, the fact that its art is made out of the virtual interaction of people with others, plus the actual interaction of the stage and the audience, make it an appropriate means of commentary upon the fabric of social intercourse from which 'states' at large are made.

In such a setting, a play's power to disturb or involve rests on the notion that, beyond the milieu depicted on the stage, there exists a 'real' material world to which it refers and on which it can impinge, somehow making a difference. Leo Reuss's sense – his outraged insistence – that, ultimately, he is not Brandhofer, even though both Reuss and Brandhofer are necessary to the realisation of Dorsday, springs from this situation. Otherwise 'Brandhofer' could simply stand as another milestone of nomenclature passed by the career of Reiss. Meanwhile, *Fräulein Else* operates – and disturbs – on a number of other levels. A paradoxical account of lust frustrated by the mode of its gratification, it casts its heroine as the central agent in a mini-drama, a 'play' located within the main action, something which the 'stream of consciousness' and feverish present-tense style of the narrative stresses. The climax of Else's 'great performance' in this drama, in which the secret prize of her nakedness eludes Dorsday by being publicly manifested, manipulates a neat, even tricky, irony, effectively neutralising Dorsday's private fantasies by externalising them. Convinced that she has none the less kept to the spirit of the appalling 'bargain', thus forcing Dorsday to save her father, Else's stratagem bids to hoist the villain with his own petard even at the cost of her life. Her sudden disrobing is thus no mere act of hysterical abandon. A histrionic gesture at once vividly accusatory and conclusively damning, it ranks as an abrupt and carefully focused assertion of moral indignation: its aim, to expose and condemn the presuppositions of its bourgeois audience through the sudden explosion in their midst of a contesting, disturbing reality.

A number of Shakespearean ghosts crowd on to the stage at such a moment. At the level of the plot, Shylock is of course readily discernible. But if we take into account Reuss's own situation, the figure of the Prince of Denmark is also hard to ignore. Like him, Reuss is using a play as a stratagem to pierce in the name of justice what he perceives as wholesale political and moral corruption: a move that aims to authenticate in the process his own 'real' identity and being. However, such a project also contains the possibility that *Hamlet* considers: that the audience may respond with blankness, as Claudius does to *The Mousetrap*. In the event, in the performance of *Fräulein Else*, this blankness occurs on two levels; that of the play's world and, as we know, that of its spectators. Not only is the response of Else's 'audience' to her nakedness in the hotel's music room one of nullity and bewilderment, but that of the Viennese audience present at the play's performance is evidently of a similar sort. Confronted by an almost naked revelation of the effect of the Nazi race-laws, their response is – nothing. Nobody asks about Reuss.

Unlike Hamlet's, Reuss's victory seems thus only a pyrrhic one. His role as Dorsday, a man in pursuit of nakedness, is ironically only available to him when he's cloaked as another, 'Brandhofer'. The story of *Fräulein Else*, on this showing, is scarcely a vehicle for self-authentication. Rather, as the social product of a role-playing society, it seems to end by celebrating precisely that: role-playing itself. Perhaps the situation implies, at least in terms of a Jewish perception of the Viennese world at the time, that that is all there is. Role-playing is a common-enough theme in the work of Schnitzler, to say nothing of Freud. The imminent rise of Hitler would crudely confirm its tragic potency. The Holocaust would savagely lay bare its implications.

In *Hamlet*, on the other hand, the sudden defeat of audience expectation in fact turns out to be a powerful weapon. Its effect is sharply to increase awareness of the material presence of the play, the audience, and thus of the volatile relationship between the two. Far from being simply negative, Claudius's blankness turns out, as we have seen, to offer nothing less than the most explosive and indeed subversive of reactions. Suddenly the whole forward motion of the action shudders to a halt, and we hear the play speak. What it seems to say is that drama doesn't always work: that the easy prognostications about guilt's self-revelation are unreliable, that with creatures as complex and as dangerously attractive as Claudius, the aim of holding a mirror up to nature is not readily achieved, that the pathway from art to 'real life' is by no means as direct and untrammelled as was sentimentally claimed, and that art's writ does not run easily in this corrupt and recognisably modern world of Elsinore. Here, as we its inheritors know all too well, one may still smile and smile and be a villain. Plays make nothing happen.

The bald, confirming truth is that the Prince succeeds in his aim despite *The Mousetrap*. Perhaps he does so even because of its failure. Certainly, as Polonius discovers, from that moment on Hamlet is prepared to use daggers as well as to speak them. For Reuss, as for any European Jew for whom Nazi persecution brought only the deadly response of nothingness, and finally its shocking material climax, *vernichtung*, *Hamlet* might well seem to be a play about the violent, murderous stratagems necessary to counter that peculiarly modern kind of corruption that takes the form of inertia, of wilful blankness, of refusal to see. It might well seem to be about the need for a different kind of art: one that sets out to seize the initiative, to harry, cajole, persuade and coerce its audience into some sort of redemptive action. And it might well be thought to speak of a Shakespeare who must, in the present and in the future, operate less as the passive Sweet William of romantic legend, and more as the intervening, directing, policing Old Bill appropriate to a harsher reality.

That surely is the Shakespeare invoked and given a clear political job to do in Berlin in 1945. As OMGUS began its mammoth, Fortinbras-like task amid the rubble, clearing the stage, taking up the bodies, its soldiers must have uncovered many ironies. Few could have matched those embodied in the fateful 'black' and 'white' lists administered by the Theatre Officers. Their source is thus a matter of considerable interest. It lay in a letter, written from Hollywood, California, by a group of German-Jewish *émigrés*, in response to a request from the Office of War Information in Washington, DC. Its controlling, marshalling purpose is baldly stated: to employ the German theatre henceforth as 'an instrument of reeducation'.[16] Perhaps even the Prince of Denmark would have agreed that the letter's main signatory, and thus the instrument of *Hamlet*'s entry as policeman into a fresh world order, might now be hailed as one of the Bard's first presentist critics. Playing what turned out, in the end, to be his most influential role, it was Lionel Royce.

6
Harry Hunks, Superstar

'One must accept the baptism of the gutter'
(W.B. Yeats)

Masters of the Game

It was a remarkable spectacle:

> The next was that a number of men and women came
> forward from a separate compartment, dancing, conversing
> and fighting with each other: also a man who threw some
> white bread among the crowd, that scrambled for it. Right
> over the middle of the place a rose was fixed, this rose
> being set on fire by a rocket: suddenly lots of apples and
> pears fell out of it down upon the people standing below.
> Whilst the people were scrambling for the apples, some
> rockets were made to fall down upon them out of the rose,
> which caused a great fright but amused the spectators.
> After this, rockets and other fireworks came flying out of
> all corners, and that was the end of the play.[1]

This, surely, is one of those great Elizabethan public spectacles with its characteristic deployment of complex pageantry: the climax of a royal masque perhaps, or the end of some theatrical display full of emblems. In fact, it describes the climax of an afternoon of bloody, flesh-rending horror at the Paris Garden in London in 1584. The spectators had been watching 'bear-baiting'. Yet, oddly, the passage uses the term 'play'.[2]

Bear-baiting was an institution in Britain, at its peak when Shakespeare was writing. Said to have its roots in classical antiquity, it seems to have existed in London almost continuously from the twelfth century. Special buildings devoted to it stood in the capital before any theatres were built and an established position of royal 'bearward' can be traced back to 1484. During the reign of Henry VIII, the 'Mastership' of the royal bears, bulls and dogs was established as a court office, and remained so throughout Shakespeare's lifetime.

Of course there were protests against the practice, often expressed in terms with which we, in the twenty-first century, would readily sympathise. Most vocal were Puritans and Protestants, but there is no doubt that their objections expressed a broader and long-standing revulsion. In 1550, Robert Crowley denounced bear-baiting as 'a full ugly sight'. Philip Stubbes, who condemns bear-baiting as 'a filthie, stinkyng and lothsome game', makes his case in terms that, with some adjustments, most moderns would not fail to approve:

> What Christian herte can take pleasure to see one poore beast to rent, teare and kill an other, and all for his foolish pleasure. And althogh thei be bloudy beasts to mankind, and seeke his destruction, yet wee are not to abuse them, for his sake who made them, and whose creatures thei are. For notwithstanding that thei be evill to us, and thirst after our bloud, yet are thei good creatures in their own nature and kind, and made to set forth the glorie, power, and magnificence of our God, and for our use, and therefore for his sake we ought not to abuse them ... And to be plaine, I think that the Devill is Maister of the Game, Beareward and all.[3]

Many Protestant clergy, with less extreme views on all manner of other matters, expressed similar sentiments and the funda-

mental arguments that sustain our own attitude were freely cir-
culating. Some municipalities, such as Chester, had prohibited
bear-baiting as early as 1596.[4] Of course, paradoxes abound in
this sort of area. As Keith Thomas points out, pamphlets
against cock-fighting were not infrequently bound up in calf-
skin.[5] But it is not merely the degree of Sabbatarian zeal that
proves intriguing about objections such as those made by
Edward Hake in his *News Out Of Powles Churchyarde* (1579):

> What else but gaine and money gote
> Maintains each Saboth day
> The bayting of the Beare and Bull?
> What brings this brutish play?[6]

It is – once more – the use of the word 'play'.

Star Wars

We would of course regard bear-baiting as belonging to a quite
different, indeed opposite, category. The chaining to a stake
and the whipping of a blinded bear was part of the spectacle.
The use of specially trained dogs to tear the bear's flesh as each
'course' proceeded guaranteed violent mutilation and plenty of
blood, guts and noise: the screaming of bears and audience was
widely reported as deafening. The German Paul Hentzner's
account of a visit to London makes no bones about the nature
of the 'entertainment' on offer:

> There is still another place, built in the form of a theatre,
> which serves for the baiting of bears and bulls. They are fas-
> tened behind, and then worried by those great English
> dogs and mastiffs, but not without great risk to the dogs
> from the teeth of the one and the horns of the other; and
> it sometimes happens they are killed upon the spot. Fresh
> ones are immediately supplied in the places of those that
> are wounded or tired. To this entertainment there often
> follows that of whipping a blinded bear, which is per-
> formed by five or six men, standing in a circle with whips,
> which they exercise upon him without any mercy.
> Although he cannot escape from them because of his
> chain, he nevertheless defends himself, vigorously throwing

down all who come within his reach and are not active
enough to get out of it, tearing the whips out of their
hands and breaking them.[7]

But far from being the resort of a vicious-minded few, this was
regarded as a 'pleasant sport' by the many, among them precisely the sort of people, aristocrats as well as commoners, who
would also visit the theatres to see 'plays' of the other kind. On
7 September 1601, the Duc de Biron was taken to the Bear
Garden by no less a host than Sir Walter Raleigh.[8] Both Queen
Elizabeth I and King James I – enthusiastic patrons of the
drama – actively supported bear-baiting and a reasonable case
can be made that the circular structure of the large public
theatres was copied from that of the bear-baiting ring.[9] Paul
Hentzner's evidently horrified reference to a 'place, built in
the form of a theatre' draws attention to that disturbing conjunction. As if to confirm it, Norden's map of London made in
1593 shows two adjacent and almost indistinguishable round
buildings laconically labelled 'The Beare howse' in one case
and 'The Play howse' in the other.

Some theatrical entrepreneurs, such as Philip Henslowe and
Edward Alleyn, even divided their time more or less equally
between the two activities.[10] Certainly, from 1594 on, in the
midst of other theatrical involvements, they paid £40 a year for
a licence to bait bears, and in November 1604, after a series of
unsuccessful bids and a payment of £450, they were finally
appointed royal Masters and Keepers of bears, bulls and dogs.
They held this post jointly until Henslowe's death in 1616, after
which Alleyn continued as sole Master.[11]

With accommodation for a thousand spectators and an
entrance fee of one penny, the bear-baiting arenas such as the
Bear Garden or Paris Garden (known to Ben Jonson as 'Beares
Colledge') offered the nearby theatres serious competition.
The rowdiness of the Bear Garden may have contributed to its
collapse in 1583, but it was rebuilt with such success that,
recording the profits at the Fortune Theatre and the Bear
Garden over the Christmas period of 1608, Henslowe's Diary
reveals that the baitings yielded substantially more than the
playhouse.[12] In 1614, after the Globe Theatre had burnt down,
Henslowe finally took the obvious course, producing a building
that could cope with both activities. Opening in October of

that year, the Hope Theatre featured a moveable stage, which enabled it, says its contract, to be 'fitt and convenient in all thinges, both for players to playe in and for the game of Bears and Bulls to be bayted in the sayme.'[13]

Global warming

Harry Hunks was one of the famous bears regularly 'baited' in arenas such as this. His human name and the hint of a recognisable 'personality' makes it difficult for us to comprehend the attraction of his regular, carefully staged whipping. But Dekker's account of this highly popular diversion remains both insistent and chilling:

> At length a blind bear was tied to the stake, and instead of baiting him with dogs, a company of creatures that had the shapes of men and faces of Christians (being either colliers, carters or watermen) took the office of beadles upon them, and whipped Monsieur Hunkes till the blood ran down his old shoulders.
>
> (Dekker, *Work for Armourers*, 1609)[14]

Beyond such horrors, such a spectacle confronts us, surely, with a serious problem. For there's more than a hint in the situation that Harry Hunks, together with no less humanly named creatures such as Tom of Lincoln, Sackerson, George Stone, Harry of Tame, Little Bess of Bromley, Don Jon, Blind Robin, Ned Whiting, Ned of Canterbury and others, ranked as genuine 'stars' in the one arena as much as any of the actors in the other.[15] One worrying conclusion must be that the two kinds of 'play', drama and bear-baiting, occupied the same frame of reference on the Bankside, with the Globe Theatre part of an ensemble of places of entertainment whose constituent parts are difficult, if not impossible, to unpick. Indeed, in Wenceslas Hollar's 'long view' of London (1647), the engraving carelessly reverses the captions on two buildings, with the result that the bear-baiting house is labelled 'The Globe' and vice versa. The force of such circumstances seems to urge that the fame of 'Hunkes of the Beare-garden', as he was known, made him in every sense a match for Burbage of the other place.[16]

Our notion of a fundamental opposition between 'drama'

on the one hand and 'bear-baiting' on the other derives from nothing in the essential nature of these activities. By and large, it is our own, modern idea of what a 'play' is that produces the notion of bear-baiting as its opposite: a horrific 'sport', with values completely opposed to those of the theatre. Our ordering of those activities, our notion that drama belongs in one category because it involves the aesthetic subtleties of art, whilst bear-baiting belongs in another because it involves the savage crudities of physical violence, would certainly not have made sense to the average member of an early modern audience. The Puritan enemies of both kinds of 'play' seemed unwilling to distinguish between them, and not infrequently damned them together. In 1583 the Lord Mayor of London wrote to Sir Francis Walsingham, concerned as so often with the spreading of the plague and the galvanising effect on that of 'one very great and dangerous inconuenience, the assemblie of people to playes, beare bayting, fencers, and prophane spectacles at the Theatre and Curtaine and other like places'.[17] From the 1590s into the next century, various Privy Council minutes and proclamations casually link 'May gaimes, morryce daunces, plaies' with 'bearbaytinges' and other 'disordered or unlawful exercises' as infractions of the Sabbath and a source of infection.[18] Stubbes's *Anatomie of Abuses* places 'Beare bayting' squarely amongst 'Stage-plays', 'May Games', 'Football', 'Readyng of wicked bookes'.[19] Thomas Dekker's sarcasm reinforces the same connection when he comments that, while the playhouses stand empty, 'the company of the Beares hold together still; they play their Tragicomedies as lively as ever they did.'[20] After complaints that, performing every day, 'the players do use to recite their plays to the great hurt and destruction of the game of bear-baiting and like pastimes', the Privy Council required that their opening hours be integrated: the theatres were required to close on Thursdays and Sundays, days which were then set aside for bear-baiting.[21]

Wholly to separate the theatres and plays from bear-baiting thus risks reducing the Globe to a cold abstraction of its larger and more complex social role. We have to accept that at least part of the audience that responded intelligently and with sensitivity to, say, *A Midsummer Night's Dream*, or *Macbeth* or *King Lear*, and that thus made those creations possible, consisted of people who also liked to see a blind and screaming Harry

Hunks whipped until he bled. The logic of this position must be to include bear-baiting in a coherent ensemble and to put into question the practice of prising plays out of it for special attention.[22] Confronting such a proposal, we encounter a (to us) disturbing relationship that not only goes to the savage heart of Shakespeare's work but raises questions about what wrenching it from its intertextual ligaments has done to the notion of 'playing' itself.

Listening to the bears

A number of features connects the experience of audiences at the 'bear-house' with those at the play-house: both activities promote a sense of 'comunal' identity in that the physical structure of the arena makes its members aware of themselves as spectators, their sense of individual or personal involvement submerged in a setting that invites or requires the display of 'public' or group responses. In that situation, the audience also reacts to itself, sensing itself as an aspect of the action, an element involved in the 'play' as part of its very fabric.[23] And at the centre of both spectacles, the focus of attention, there throbs a 'live', unpredictable quality of immediacy in the sense that both seem to frame, manage and work with contingency, with unshaped, actual, 'here and now' experience, making that a fundamental part of what they have to offer. In this sense both events seem categorisable as 'games' – bear-baiting's unpredictability makes it possible to 'play' or bet on the outcome – and that expanded sense of the concept must in turn be part of what is hinted at by the early modern term 'play'.

Any analysis of that will demand what Clifford Geertz calls – borrowing the notion from the British philosopher Gilbert Ryle – 'thick description': a focus on the symbolic dimension of social actions which aims to place them in the context of the cultures in which they occur and to construe them as events whose raw content (available in 'thin' description) is ultimately overridden by a larger semantic function. Such activities do not 'mean' in themselves. It is *we* who mean, by them. For an early modern audience, the questions remain pressing. To what dimensions of their imaginative universe did the bear-garden speak? What did they mean by the spectacle of a blind and bleeding Harry Hunks?

Some clues perhaps lie in the extent to which tormenting the bears could be felt to inhabit the same category as other forms of public 'baiting'. Just as at the bear-garden, audiences at the stocks, the pillory, the scaffold and the whipping post were not discouraged from active vocal and even physical participation in the spectacular harassment of a centrally displayed figure.[24] Together with the custom of the hobby-horse, or charivari, they contributed to an ancient and continuing public tradition of retributive entertainment.[25] As Meredith Ann Skura notes, these can all be said to constitute the 'same kind of sport' as bear-baiting: displays that, by 'show-casing' the guilty, function as a method of 'policing' or of social control.[26] She makes the point that bear-baiting was not the only type of public enactment in which the performer was a victim and the performance deadly. The cycle of mystery plays inevitably culminated in the baiting and crucifixion of Christ, and the public stages had always offered the more generalised spectacle of the actor surrounded by an audience whose response could at any moment descend to hissing and abuse.[27] Certainly it could be argued that public remonstrance, the direction of a punitive collective gaze, presents us with the founding form of what we like to think of as 'entertainment' in early modern society, and that some form of 'baiting' lies at its source.

Lore and ordure

Surprisingly, certain aspects of Geertz's account of the Balinese cock-fight might also prove relevant.[28] Geertz points out that the cock-fight works in terms of distinct binary opposites: an untamed, unpredictable animal fury confronts but is also framed and secured within a set of sophisticated, socially authenticated rules and regulations. Like the cock, the bear also carries implications of a free-ranging animality, of which rampant and unrestrained sexuality is a significant aspect. Inevitably soliciting restriction, this quality simultaneously also invites tentative, and potentially explosive, engagement. In both contests, an untrammelled 'nature' thus confronts a prophylactic, moderating 'culture', whose laws both provoke and restrain it. Although the term 'hunks' was traditionally used of ill-tempered, surly old persons who could not unreasonably be thought of as 'bears', the figure of the bear in Western European and North American folk-tale has also always carried with it a sense of uninhibited natural force (William Faulkner's story 'The Bear' continues this tradition into the twentieth century). In this context, it belongs to that half-submerged misty sphere of myth, folk-belief, custom and practice called 'lore'. It is perhaps no accident that the modern Anglo-American concept of freewheeling male sexuality employs the term 'hunk'.

Undoubtedly, at some level, bear-baiting acts out the mastery of human culture over an unredeemed 'natural' world. The spectacle of a man whipping a bear reassures its spectators of that whilst exhibiting, or deliberately courting, the penalties that undermining such dominance might bring. Nevertheless, it is also salutary to deconstruct the grounding terms of the opposition. After all, there is no 'nature' in the innocent, transparent, unmediated sense that it seems to imply. The savagery that early modern society feels itself to be confronting is a product of its own culture and sheds its own revealing light on some of that culture's presuppositions and concerns. As we move closer to it, rather more specific dimensions appear, offering to reflect those presuppositions and concerns with a greater precision.

In fact, the smell and the savagery, the blood and the guts that characterise the bear-garden seem only to become most fully and fruitfully meaningful in terms of an opposition whose other binary term wants firmly to authenticate human behaviour as rational, calculable and rule-bound. As a result, bear-baiting generates meaning most effectively when opposed not – as we would see it – to the modes and values endorsed by the theatre, but to those of a very different institution. The polarity at stake operates clearly in an epigram coined by Sir John Davies in 1594:

> Publius, student at the common law,
> Oft leaves his books, and for his recreation,
> To Paris Garden doth himself withdraw,
> Where he is ravished with such delectation,
> As down among the bears and dogs he goes;
> Where, whilst he skipping cries, 'To head! to head!',
> His satin doublet and his velvet hose
> Are all with spittle from above bespread:
> When he is like his father's country hall,

> Stinking with dogs and muted all with hawks;
> And rightly on him too this filth doth fall,
> Which for such filthy sports his books forsakes;
> Leaving old Ployden, Dyer, Brooke alone,
> To see old Harry Hunks and Sacarson.[29]

Here the 'game', represented by its most formidable stars, stands in clear and defining opposition to the formalised institution of the law, represented in its abstract, academic mode by the written works of its most authoritative expositors. The cultural logic involved is surely impeccable, even though its conclusions may strike us as strange. Bear-baiting belongs to and evokes a pre-literate, oral sphere of concrete, unanalysed custom, myth and folk-tale – of 'lore' – to which a written, abstract, codified, rationally based set of equivalences and injunctions – a reified 'law' – must inevitably be opposed.[30] Metaphorically, but no less powerfully, the 'order' computed, endorsed, and prescribed by that law and the sort of 'colledge' at which Publius studies it stands in meaningful opposition to the 'ordure' – the excremental 'filth' – that, indiscriminately 'muted' and falling on the truant student at the 'Beares Colledge', signals the material imperatives of life at their most fundamental.

The public theatre's own involvement with that 'ordure', with the actual 'spittle' and 'filth' of unstructured material existence, links it firmly in such a setting to bear-baiting. Both 'bear-house' and 'play-house' are perceived as dealing in the oral opposite of an abstract, academic and written-down law, and are defined by that. Ben Jonson's nomination of Paris Garden as 'Beares Colledge' generates an intense irony from exactly that opposition. In fact, on 31 October 1614, the Lady Elizabeth's company production of Jonson's *Bartholomew Fair* was amongst the first offerings of the newly constructed, dual-purpose, bear-baiting and play-producing Hope Theatre. The smell of the bears and of their ordure was said to give the building – interestingly termed the 'plaie house or game house' – a not inappropriate whiff of Smithfield market, where the play was set, and reference is duly made in it to the 'Stage-keeper's' task of 'sweeping the stage, or gathering up the broken apples for the bears within' (*Bartholomew Fair*, Induction, 65–6). The play's Induction records the presence of exactly the sort of filth and smells that afflicted Publius: the arena is 'as dirty as Smith-field, and as stinking every whit' (*Bartholomew Fair*, Induction, 208–9). Its satire begins appropriately with the laborious reading of a spurious legal document giving details of the 'Art-icles of agreement, indented between the spectators or hearers at the Hope on the Bankside in the county of Surrey on the one party' and the play's author on the other. Derision of this complexity evidently commits the theatre – along with the great London Fair itself – to a set of just-discernible distinctions from which cultural meaning may thence unthinkingly be spun.

Out to play

There are, of course, a number of moments in Shakespeare's plays when bear-baiting is casually mentioned – as when Slender in *Merry Wives*, who loves the sport, especially when the bear breaks loose, boasts that he has caught Sackerson 'twenty times' (1.1.266), or when Andrew Aguecheek bemoans his fondness for its distractions (*Twelfth Night*, 1.3.92). Alexander Leggatt makes the telling point that '...there are passages where Shakespeare, consciously or not, gives the action a struc-ture and rhythm like that of a bearbaiting'. He is referring to those moments when a single figure is set on by a group of antagonists, and he points to *Timon of Athens*, *Richard III*, and a wide range of other instances.[31]

But a considerable distance separates these characters and moments from a series of more complex, messy occasions when something quite specific, but less readily definable, seems to become part of the process of 'playing'. An important clue as to the complexities implied by the term perhaps lies here. It becomes palpable in certain moments of performance when an apparently ungovernable and unruly uncontrollable range of 'here and now' or 'real world' experience seems suddenly to be deliberately solicited, sought out or provoked from within the 'play world' of the text. The result is a kind of eruption, which, uncontrolled and unpredictable, seems momentarily to flare up from the stage. The report of the 'play' with which we began, with its astonishing fireworks and the bursting rose that showers apples and pears onto the audience, can stand as an apt symbol for the process. Instantly dissolving whatever separates the play from the auditorium, such moments suddenly and alarmingly launch out into the audience, overwhelming, embracing, splashing and muddying it like any violent piece of 'brutish play' in a bear-pit. At such moments, we seem almost to catch the text doing overtly what texts more usually do covertly: provoking, engaging with, moulding, constructing and modifying inchoate experience, which – as a result of that intervention – begins to signify. We can call it making meaning.

A simple example might be the brief but shocking transformation, irrevocably darkening the comedy, that surges from the stage when Malvolio's final cry 'I'll be revenged on the whole pack of you' suddenly turns him into a whipped, tortured bear, beset by baiting dogs. That the audience simultaneously and disconcertingly experiences itself as part of that hounding pack adds to the effect.[32] Something similar seeps from the figure of Coriolanus when, covered in blood, and fighting off assailants of all kinds, he ringingly and disturbingly dismisses them as 'You common cry of curs'. A cognate feature becomes – in Macbeth's lines

> They have tied me to a stake; I cannot fly,
> But bearlike I must fight the course.
>   (5.7.1–2)

– almost the very source of their complex, shaming power.

In *King Lear*, the torturing of Gloucester in full view of the audience uses the technical terms of the 'game' to moralise the horror accompanying the gouging out of his eyes: 'I am tied to the stake and I must stand the course' (11.7.53). But this by no means exhausts the bear-baiting connection in that play, which starts to emerge much earlier in the case of Edmund. His self-defining speech in Act 1 (when the play is still only minutes old), presents a highly persuasive justification of unencumbered carnality; of a powerful sexual energy confined by no cultural restrictions:

> Thou, nature art my goddess; to thy law
> My services are bound. Wherefore should I
> Stand in the plague of custom, and permit
> The curiosity of nations to deprive me,
> For that I am some twelve or fourteen moonshines

Lag of a brother? Why bastard? Wherefore base?
When my dimensions are as well compact,
My mind as generous and my shape as true
As honest madam's issue? Why brand they us
With base? With baseness? Bastardy? Base? Base?
Who, in the lusty stealth of nature, take
More composition and fierce quality
Than doth, within a dull, stale, tired bed,
Go to th' creating a whole tribe of fops
Got 'tween asleep and wake?

                                                (1.2.1–15)

This is truly the voice of a 'hunk'. Yet the slightest taste developing in us for Edmund's disarming, bear-like vigour turns into the very factor that empowers his evil. The fleeting disorder that erupts brings with it the smack of another arena.

Larger dimensions appear, needless to say, in the play that contains a bear, *The Winter's Tale*. It opens with the figure of the courtier Archidamus, apparently developing a conversation that has already begun. Yet, seconds later, his confident flow suddenly falters:

> Verily I speak it in the freedom of my knowledge: we cannot with such magnificence – in so rare – I know not what to say...
>
>   (1.1.11–13)

What is the audience to make of a point in a play when an actor, apparently stumbling in his speech, abruptly says 'I know not what to say...'. As we have seen in the case of Polonius in *Hamlet*, the scene seems momentarily to spin out of control, as the play-world topples over into the audience's world, and a well-spoken character all at once turns into a fumbling actor who may have forgotten his lines. Although Archidamus quickly recovers, 'loss of control' has by these means been established as one of the major issues raised by 'playing', and the point is frequently reinforced from now on. In Act 2, at the peak of one of his rantings about Hermione's unfaithfulness, Leontes interrupts his accusations with the stumbling 'oh I am out!' (2.1.72), a phrase that again suggests that the actor playing the part has got his lines wrong. Similar moments proliferate, in which the play's language suddenly and disconcertingly manages to vault the barriers separating the stage from the world beyond.[33] Most remarkably, Leontes starts to pick at the seams of 'playing' itself when, gesturing across the stage to where Hermione and Polixenes are silently talking, he launches into an account of their behaviour as startling in its immediacy as it is pointed in its implications:

> Too hot, too hot!
> To mingle friendship far is mingling bloods.
> I have *tremor cordis* on me; my heart dances,
> But not for joy, not joy...
> [...]
> But to be paddling palms and pinching fingers
> As now they are, and making practised smiles
> As in a looking glass...
>
> (1.2.108ff.)

What shocks here is not only the sense of a commentary that is already beginning to lap at the stage's edge, as it remarks on the very process of 'playing' – 'making practised smiles / As in a looking glass' – but the stunning immediacy of phrases like 'as *now* they are'. These astonishingly urge the audience to look in a particular direction, here and now, in the theatre, and to react in a specific way, whilst – because of the stress on the artificiality of acting – making them simultaneously suspicious of what they see and the responses they have. This manipulation of the present moment makes us unsure whether we are watching actors 'playing' in the sense that they are transparently representing human behaviour, or, as Leontes urges, noticing that they are playing 'acting' and thus drawing attention to the nuts and bolts of the art that holds them and the play together.

The disarray which this degree of immediacy cannot help but foster in an audience finds itself further and further exploited as the meaningful structures of the language begin drastically to break down. Ultimately, it reaches a point where the disintegration starts to carry well beyond the story. 'Playing' itself begins to be torn at, ferociously and, unsurprisingly, it starts to unravel:

    Gone already!
Inch-thick, knee-deep, oe'r head and ears a forked one!
Go play, boy, play, thy mother plays, and I
Play too, but so disgraced a part, whose issue
Will hiss me to my grave; contempt and clamour
Will be my knell. Go play, boy, play.

(1.2.185–7)

At this juncture, a modern audience might well sense a notion of 'playing' at stake, to some of whose dimensions we no longer have access. For, having once more drawn attention to the process of acting, indeed having presented himself as a bear-like actor figure, hissed at by jeering spectators, the actor playing Leontes abruptly and alarmingly turns his attention to the auditorium he faces here and now. He starts to speak directly, and, as he insists, in the present moment, to specific members of the audience who are standing there and watching him:

    There have been,
Or I am much deceived, cuckolds ere now,
And many a man there is, even at this present,
Now, while I speak this, holds his wife by th'arm,
That little thinks she has been sluiced in his absence,
And his pond fished by his next neighbour, by
Sir Smile, his neighbour.

(1.2.189–96)

The impact of this comes not only from the unpleasant imagery, but from what is now a quite vehement and disturbing immediacy, reinforced by an insistent and alarming deixis: 'even at this present, / Now, while I speak this'. 'Playing', pitched at this level of intensity, might well make an audience feel that it has been splashed with ordure. Riding the wave of the preceding references to language, the bombshells land not only at the feet of an actual unsuspecting audience member and his no doubt nervously smiling wife; their blast quickly extends to his grinning neighbour. Suddenly, the play bursts the conventions of its own art and explodes with 'presentist' energy into the here-and-now material life of its spectators. Projecting itself beyond the written script, as beyond the stage, it

seizes embarrassed spectators by the scruff of the neck, dragging them into the action and making their response part of
the event. Such gestures invoke the 'brutish play' of bear-
baiting and its capacity to involve an audience by splattering
and staining it, as much as any politer, Hamlet-derived notions
of the methods and purpose of 'playing'.

A similar situation occurs right at the end of the play, at one
of its most famous moments. Leontes finds himself confronted
by a statue of his dead wife, Hermione. Through the 'magic'
apparently administered by Paulina, the statue moves and
descends from its pedestal. A 'lawful' spell (5.3.105) makes it –
to Leontes and the audience – lifelike. Then, in an astonishing
coup de théâtre, Leontes stretches out his hand to touch the
stone and utters the words that indicate to the audience, who
have also not been privy to Paulina's deception, that the statue
is in fact Hermione herself:

> Oh, she's warm!
>   (5.3.109)

Once again, an event on the stage floods into the audience, as
Leontes's surprise seems to breach the boundaries of 'playing'
to generate and record the audience's surprise too. Little in
the story has prepared us for this since, like Leontes, we have
been persuaded that Hermione is dead. We may also have pre-
sumed that, since the 'statue' is so lifelike, it could have readily
been 'played' by the actor who plays the dead queen. But the
announcement that the statue is in fact alive breaks that convention wide open and allows it to reach beyond the stage to
embrace us. Leontes's next words, emphasising the ultimately
'lawful' nature of such 'magic', prove to be amongst the most
memorable of the play:

> If this be magic, let it be an art
> Lawful as eating.
>   (5.3.110–11)

In the very act of invoking the law, these lines hint at realms of
activity whose nature undermines the pretensions of legal com-
putation. 'Eating' challenges – in effect swallows – the concept
of a codifiable lawfulness because the ingestion of sustenance

stands as a precondition of existence, of life itself. 'Eating' must precede any abstract legal calculus and thus invokes a concept of 'lawfulness' so broad as to be undistinctive. An art that is as 'Lawful as eating' is no art at all and can only fall into the category we lamely term 'nature', where the human distinctions of 'lawful' and 'unlawful' don't apply. This is the realm of what the play terms 'great creating Nature' (4.4.88) where the inchoate contingency characteristic of 'playing' rules. What is taking place on the stage at this point seems to offer itself – by leaping beyond the stage – as just such a 'natural' activity. It's a notion of art well beyond the presuppositions of our own world.

'Eating' may be an apt symbol for it, though its relevance to the theatre is not immediately evident. In this play, the law at its most unyielding and vindictive – distilled to a cruel 'rigour' (3.2.112) – has already been seen in action at Hermione's trial. Formally arraigned, accused of 'high treason', she experiences the law as exactly that written, abstract, reified system of calculated equivalences that the incalculable turmoil of bear-baiting challenges and undermines.[34] Yet, famously, *The Winter's Tale* is also a play in which, as part of the 'magic' or 'art' that redeems human sinfulness, indeed right in the middle of the action, at the point where that redemption begins, a bear appears who proceeds to eat a human being.[35]

The creature's alarming on-stage manifestation certainly brings with it a broad challenge to the atmosphere of arraignement, accusation, reified legality and trial that characterises Leontes's court.[36] Its off-stage 'dining' – reported with appropriate immediacy as happening 'Now, now' – becomes the pivotal occasion where a comic rustic lore at last starts to undermine by parody the inhuman savagery of the law of Leontes's court:

Clown: . . . to see how the bear tore out his shoulder-bone, how he cried to me for help, and said his name was Antigonus, a nobleman! . . . how the poor souls roared, and the sea mocked them; and how the poor gentleman roared, and the bear mocked him, both roaring louder than the sea or weather.
Shepherd: Name of mercy, when was this, boy?
Clown: Now, now; I have not winked since I saw these sights; the men are not yet cold under water, nor the bear half dined on the gentleman; he's at it now.

[...]

Shepherd: Heavy matters, heavy matters! But look thee here,
   boy. Now bless thyself; thou met'st with things dying, I with
   things new-born.

(3.3.94–113)

Here, the play seems to confirm a logic of the bear-garden and
to link it with a logic of the theatre. It is one which proposes
that, despite the opposition between human 'law' and the
'eating' associated with the bears, another level exists at which
such 'eating' may be perceived as 'natural' and therefore not
only positioned at the frontiers of culture and law, but –
because of that location – as definitive of and so fundamental
to what divides them. That is, both bear-garden and theatre
offer a way of negotiating a contradiction built into the notion
of codifiable law: that despite the claims for universal validity
that its prescriptions presuppose, it has both to recognise and
exclude a 'nature' to which it does not apply. The bear-garden
and *The Winter's Tale* both offer a kind of lawful/unlawful art in
which this paradox can be resolved: in which, as nature
embraces art, and as eating may be recuperated as lawful, so
tragedy may even be redeemed as comedy, the dead reclaimed
for life.

We need not dwell on this bear. The figure who most
decisively straddles the 'lawful–unlawful' or 'law–lore' polarity
in the play is of course Autolycus. A representative of those
'masterless' men whom early modern culture most deeply mis-
trusted, he lives beyond the law. Untroubled by society's restrictions and hierarchies, Autolycus is someone who, by his own
account, 'having flown over many knavish professions' has
'settled only in rogue' (4.3.101). His roots in that world locate
him well outside the range of the idealised pastoral glow suffus-
ing the relationship of Florizel and Perdita. But his standing is
also more precisely delineated as a result. He enters singing
(4.3) and his thoroughgoing involvement with song and dance
means that, almost literally, he 'overflows' the stage as music
and movement inevitably do. The rhythms and harmonies he
introduces move through the theatre to invade the bodies of
spectators and listeners as ineluctably intimate, non-discursive
forces, able to operate at a physical as well as an emotional
level. As a committed 'rogue', he has already and in any case

traditional connections with the disorderly subcultural network linking the Bankside and the bear-garden beyond the theatre. In fact, his title is almost a professional designation, something reinforced in the Folio text where, in the 'Names of the Actors', he is cited simply as 'a Rogue'.[37]

It is thus unsurprising to discover, from his first song, that, in addition to an interest in eating and drinking, this embodiment of what the Acts for the punishment of Vagabondes denounced as the 'rogish kinde of lyfe' also 'haunts wakes, fairs, and bear-baitings' (4.3.102–3). His tattered apparel gives us the man: indeed, his clothing becomes an aspect of one of the play's major themes when his present stained 'caparison', remarkable for its dilapidation, provides the means by which he tricks his first victim. These 'detestable things' also become, as Florizel's disguise, one of the main devices by which the complex plot is resolved. Indeed, Autolycus's own acquisition of finer apparel is precisely what enables him to cross the social boundary into the world of the courtier. This haunter of bear-baitings thus also embodies one of the central nightmares of early modern orthodoxy; the rogue whose exploitation of sumptuary laws regarding dress codes enables him silently to slip the nets of caste and class.

A ready model for this sort of subversion was of course the actor. Like many other plays, *The Winter's Tale* focuses on costuming and disguise as a means of circumventing the restrictions of social hierarchy. Of course, it plays safe: the subversive potential of its own nuts-and-bolts procedures – dressing in somebody else's clothes – is on the one hand ostensibly advertised and on the other potentially defused.[38] But 'playing' a gentleman in his borrowed finery certainly suits Autolycus. He not only enjoys the spurious 'authority' it bestows, but the Clown's comment to his father seems deliberately to stimulate a specific echo:

> He seems to be of great authority: close with him, give him gold: and though authority be a stubborn bear, yet he is oft led by the nose with gold.
>
> (4.4.800–02)

Appropriately, the fake authority of this 'stubborn bear' turns out to be a much more potent agent of subversion than Perdita, particularly when her newly revealed nobility conveniently solves the problem she causes.[39] As the play ends, his raucous under-mining of law continues to thrive, unchecked. And as a focus of generalised fears concerning free-wheeling sexuality (the bawdy content of his 'love songs for maids' is graphically illustrated by the snatches we hear quoted, 4.4.191–201), as well as a reminder of authority that can be suborned, or bought, this rogueish figure almost seems to stand four-square at the play's centre, an unsettling challenge to inherited nobility, and, no doubt, in performance at the Globe, a compelling and disturbing reminder of that other, congruent arena whose stench and stains mark the costume that he wears and indeed flaunts.

Coll pixci

Meaning is made not found, and cultures characteristically deploy binary opposites to this end. Constructing differences, we construct ourselves: we are what we oppose. The central sug-gestion of this chapter is that we may, for complex historical reasons involving the pursuit of our own meanings, have slightly misconceived some of the systems of difference most powerfully at work in early modern society. The effect of that will be inevitably and systematically misleading. Thus, where we might polarise bear-baiting and drama, the Elizabethans quite clearly did not. 'Playing', and in particular its commitment to moments of hair-raising roller-coaster contingency, in which spectators and actors find themselves pitched into an incoher-ent terrain where they momentarily unite as participants, char-acterised both activities to a degree that we can only glimpse out of the corner of our collective cultural eye.

The polar opposite of this unstructured, and essentially oral, dimension lay in the sphere of the written word: in a world of book-learning and, at its heart, of the written and codified law – the world of Publius's neglected volumes of Ployden, Dyer, and Brooke.[40] Here contingency was kept at bay by a restrictive, reassuring framework of abstract tit-for-tat calculation and statute. That opposition of 'lore'–law and 'ordure'–order, just to touch on the teeming range of metaphors and puns it effort-lessly generates, seems to be concretely and potently at work in the period, however difficult it may be for us even dimly to discern it. But trying to do so will radically alter the way we per-

ceive the texts in which it operates. They should, if this suggestion has any force, start to look very different.

We can, oddly enough, put this specifically to the test in the
case of *The Winter's Tale*. For we are able, like Leontes, to
consult a rarely available oracle. It is one of those infrequent
and feared apparitions whose appearance never fails to harrow
modern scholars with fear and wonder: an eye witness.

In the Winters Talle at the glob 1611 the 15 of maye. Ɏ[41]

Obserue ther howe Lyontes the kinge of Cicillia was
overcom wth Ielosy of his wife with the kinge of Bohemia his
frind that came to see him. and howe he Contriued his
death and wold haue had his cup berer to haue poisened.
who gaue the king of bohemia warning therof & fled with
him to bohemia/

Remember also howe he sent to the Orakell of apollo &
the Aunswer of apollo. that she was giltles. and that the
king was Ielouse & c and howe Except the Child was found
Again that was loste the kinge should die wthout yssue. for
the child was caried into bohemia & ther laid in a forrest &
brought up by a sheppard. And the king of bohemia his
sonn maried that wentch & howe they fled into Cicillia to
Leontes. and the sheppard hauing showed the letter of the
noble man by whom leontes sent a was [?][42] that child and
the Iewells found about her. she was knowen to be leontes
daughter and was then 16 yers old

Remember also the Rog that cam in all tottered like coll
pixci/.[43] and howe he feyned him sicke & to have bin
Robbed of all that he had and howe he cosoned the por
man of all his money. and after cam to the shep sher with a
pedlers pack & ther cosened them Again of all ther money
And how he changed apparrell wth the king of bomia his
sonn. and then howe he turned Courtiar & c/beware of
trustinge feined beggars or fawning fellouse

The account of the play by Dr Simon Forman (1552–1611) is
usually dismissed as imperceptive, unintelligent, or obtuse. He
makes no mention of bears, of statues – of any of the grander
dimensions of the play that strike us as salient and meaningful.
Worse, Forman's credentials are not particularly impressive. A

known dabbler in necromancy and alchemy, he was repeatedly imprisoned for quackery and his case books and diaries indicate a sexual appetite whose scope and indiscriminancy offer his modern biographers little grounds for tempering a prevailing scorn.[44] Yet Forman was not stupid, as A.L. Rowse has reminded us, and this is not a version of *The Winter's Tale* that an imperceptive or unintelligent spectator would give. It reads suspiciously like the account a person might produce who literally saw something quite different from ourselves.[45]

Forman's notes on the performances he saw were collected by him in a manuscript entitled *The Bocke of Plaies and Notes thereof per Formans – for Common Policy*. As Rowse points out, in Elizabethan parlance, 'common policy' meant 'practical use'.[46] Writing, as it turned out, within days of his own death, this intensely practical early modern spectator (who more than once used a visit to the theatre to pick up a sexual partner) proved to be interested in what he could learn from the plays to apply to his own life. Hence the repeated pattern of his observations, which characteristically move from passive recording – 'Observe there ... Remember how...' – to the more intensely practical 'Beware of...'. This rhetorical structure in fact informs each of the entries Forman made concerning three separate visits to the Globe, as it clearly orders his comments on *The Winter's Tale*.

However unpromising these initially seem, their disposition of the play's parts certainly confirms the opposition between the 'law' and 'order' embodied by Leontes's machinations, and the opposed world of Autolycus. The latter's appearance as a filthy and bederaggled 'coll pixci' immediately confirms his association with the world of folktale, magic and 'lore' – to say nothing of 'ordure'. His commitment to clothes-changing is dwelt upon, and the transformation from the social level indicated by 'tottered' to that of 'Courtiar' carefully noted. But most apparent is the amount of attention given to this frequenter of bear-baitings. Autolycus takes up virtually a third of the entry, and confirms the sense of his centrality that the 'rogue' himself offers.[47] Those scornful of Forman's judgement in the matter might recall that Dr Johnson's account of the play mentions no other character but Autolycus, whom he describes as 'very naturally conceived and strongly represented'[48] The performance given by Autolycus is the one that elicits Forman's final active injunction 'beware', a decisive change of tone acknowledging fulfilment of the pursuit of 'common policy'. Appropriately, his focus is on the vivid realisation of the part on the stage and this supports the view that Autolycus was probably played by Robert Armin, the skilful and subtle clown who took over from Will Kempe in 1599.[49] It certainly seems that his powerful performance did, on this occasion, 'overflow' the stage to impinge forcefully upon at least one audience member's bosom. You can almost hear the fireworks, see the apples and pears falling.

Perhaps naturally, this account also leaves modern readers with a good deal less than they bargained for: a complicated plot, sudden jealousies, inexplicable coincidence all crammed into a creaking pastoral framework: its main and unifying interest vested in the compelling figure who enters in Act 4 – a memorable singing, dancing, clothes-changing rogue whose antics threaten the very fabric of civilisation. This is certainly not *The Winter's Tale* as we know it.

But the point of viewing the play from the perspective of Harry Hunks, as it were, can hardly be to reproduce that. Nor, it should quickly be added, is it at all possible to claim that this offers a genuine 'early modern' realignment of its features. Such authenticity is scarcely available to a viewpoint that, in its very choice of play, playwright and method of analysis, as well as in its concern to challenge an already established mapping of the terrain, betrays the interests of the late twentieth and early twenty-first centuries. Of course, as has been pointed out earlier, it can be argued that we, in the early twenty-first century, are in effect the best audience these plays could have.[50] Be that as it may, they also offer us the reverse: a no less valuable sense of material, unbridgeable difference, of the distances that truly separate us from the Shakespearean past: a sense, that is, of history.

If that fails to satisfy, a final recourse must be to words themselves. They too exist in history. It's worth remembering that a preliterate age, committed to language in its spoken form, deepens and sophisticates its communication by means of the activity of punning, something that a literate society often judges to be the lowest form of wit. In the early modern period, for instance, the term 'bait' always permitted two opposed areas of meaning to be brought into play: the straightforward sense of tormenting or persecuting, and an opposite one in which the term could also mean to 'feed' or 'rest', to 'refresh', nourish, or sustain, as in to 'bate' a horse. Maybe the bread, apples and pears strewn across the arena after a bear-baiting promote this latter sense and suggest that the occasion – like a visit to the theatre next door – was also felt to offer, after all the blood and horrors, a mitigating period of rest and recuperation, of release, of relaxation. It may be that, in making such a suggestion, this essay, like one of Publius's hawks, merely 'mutes' (i.e. defecates over) the pantheon of timeless masterpieces. But perhaps the case demands a more complex notion of *catharsis*. If so, it's not surprising that, at the Globe Theatre in London in 1611, where one of its agents was Autolycus, the other might well turn out to have been Harry Hunks.

7
Hank Cinq

Poop-poop!

He needs no introduction. In fact, the trumpeting sound of his motor car does the job all too well, perhaps too often and usually too late. The work in which he stars, Kenneth Grahame's *The Wind in the Willows*, serves consequently as his perfect context and foil. It both contains, and fails to contain, each poop! an urgent propellant projecting him beyond the text of that children's book into the realms of what we used to think of as our 'national' imagination. In this, of course, Toad is the evident heir of earlier disruptive literary characters with similar commitments to boisterous self-announcement. Sir Toby Belch, Sir John Falstaff and Bully Bottom could all be sure of a welcome at Toad Hall, where the echoes of 'poop-poop!' would mingle readily with those of 'Hem, boys!' and 'S'Blood!'. Perhaps Toad's space-and-time-defying fantasies of rocketing beyond one's earthly context –

> The poetry of motion! The *real* way to travel! The *only* way to travel! Here today – in next week tomorrow! Villages skipped, towns and cities jumped – always somebody else's horizon! O bliss! O poop-poop!...[1]

– don't quite match the superhuman projections of 'Bottom's Dream', but their inter-species trajectory is just as complex. Somehow, for both, propulsion beyond the material limits of this world breaks the bounds of humanity itself: ' "O stop being an ass, Toad!" cried the Mole despairingly.'[2]

Just before Bottom stops being an ass, an odd moment occurs in the middle of *A Midsummer Night's Dream*. He lies, with the four lovers, asleep on the stage. Theseus and Hippolyta enter, on a hunting expedition, and Theseus is hoping to impress Hippolyta with what he calls the 'musical confusion / Of hounds and echo in conjunction' (4.1.105–10). She responds, in some remarkable lines, with a memory of her own:

> I was with Hercules and Cadmus once,
> When in a wood of Crete they bay'd the bear
> With hounds of Sparta; never did I hear
> Such gallant chiding; for, besides the groves,
> The skies, the fountains, every region near
> Seem'd all one mutual cry; I never heard
> So musical a discord, such sweet thunder.
>
> (4.1.111–17)

These are beautiful lines. But if we listen carefully, there's something troubling right at the centre of them, underlying their beauty, perhaps even contributing to it. Of course, to some degree they depict what they celebrate: the sophisticated conjunction that is *concordia discors*. What's worrying, however, is a growing sense that the sounds they describe, and to some extent embody, also offer to propel us clear of the text and its overt semantic project, into the presence of something more disconcerting and less easy to verbalise. Suddenly, with that 'mutual cry', we find ourselves a long way from the acceptable braying of the comically asinine. Gradually, dimly, we can just make out, through as much as by means of the words, a rather different, shadowy, but compelling, figure. It's a bear. It's fighting for its life. Perhaps its name is 'Harry'.

There's an even odder moment in *A Midsummer Night's Dream*, which also takes place when Bottom is on the stage. It occurs in the play's last Act, given over more or less in its entirety to the mechanicals' performance of *Pyramus and Thisbe*.

Theseus commands that the Prologue should approach him, there is a flourish of trumpets, and Peter Quince enters to begin his garbled prolegomenon to the play. After a brief sally of jokes, a stage direction in the Folio text calls for the entry of Bottom (as Pyramus), Flute (as Thisbe), Snout (as Wall), Starveling (as Moonshine) and Snug (as the Lion). But as they make their entrance, we catch a fleeting glimpse of a further shadowy figure who precedes them. Once again, the effect is momentarily to pitch the audience into a realm quite beyond the words uttered in the play. For whatever that figure looks like, however he enters and walks, he advertises plainly a mode of communication over and above that of the verbal. He is carrying a trumpet. His name is William.

Harry Hunks is, we know, the name of the famous fighting bear whose professional domain centres on the arena standing virtually next door to the Globe Theatre. That his virtual presence flickers briefly in *A Midsummer Night's Dream* supports the argument, if support is needed, that it's not materially possible wholly to separate those theatres and plays from bear-baiting. Their conjunction, as has been argued earlier, is precisely what thickens the early modern sense of 'playing', and Harry Hunks's (or any bear's) momentary chimerical appearance in Hippolyta's speech, together with that of a murderous pack of dogs, is testimony to a *A Midsummer Night's Dream*'s complex role in its own culture, and a warning against reducing the Globe to a simplified abstraction of its function in ours.

The Folio stage direction 'Tawyer with a Trumpet before them', which announces the entry of Bottom and his troupe, refers specifically to William Tawyer, an actor in the company, and it marks for him a brief and unique moment of glory, in which he's named as a participant in one of the Bard's most famous plays. His role – this is all it consists of, unless he doubles with another part – is an interesting one. It doesn't require him to be able to play the trumpet, but the fact that he leads the actors onto the stage none the less firmly associates Bottom and his colleagues with some degree of celebratory pooping. In fact, Tawyer's appearance could be the basis of a particular kind of 'gag'. If the initial 'flourish' of trumpets sounded off-stage had been sufficiently elaborate, then the appearance – apparently as its source – of a halting, wilting figure, possessed of a battered instrument, at the head of these appalling actors might generate some mildly surprised laughter, as well as being appropriate to their grandiose pretensions. And it would of course help if Tawyer was already known to the audience, from past performances in the repertory, as an available figure of fun.

But Tawyer's trumpet also has a further dimension. Indeed, its musical mode of communication links him to an expanded, nondiscursive and non-textual notion of stage performance whose roots reach to a level far deeper than that plumbed by any modern drama. In essence, Tawyer's trumpet hints at a non-verbal 'performative' dimension of public display, which our notion of the play as a written 'text' has systematically, over the years, obscured from us. As Robert Weimann has powerfully argued, the tension between that older inheritance and a newly emerging text-based notion of drama, the grounding of the one we inherit, is clearly evident in many documents of the period. The protest – made as late as 1615 – against the practices of one kind of 'Common Player' catches its essence:

> When he doth hold conference vpon the stage; and should looke directly in his fellows face; hee turnes about his voice into the assembly for applause-sake, like a Trumpeter in the fields, that shifts places to get an eccho.[3]

The non-discursive potential of the trumpet preceding the mechanicals' entrance thus immediately announces a significant dimension of their 'rudeness'. Its potential poop! – as with the screams of a bear at bay – impels the audience once more beyond the play's words very much in the same spirit with which we know and expect that Bottom and his men will habitually leap beyond the text of *Pyramus and Thisbe*. In other words, its putative blast announces their production as one rooted in an inherited, preliterate performative tradition, which Shakespeare's play in its turn both confronts and tries to contain. As its bearer, Tawyer mutely embodies and champions a doomed, but still powerful, force.

State of play

Four hundred years on, the figures of William Tawyer and Harry Hunks, symbols of the propulsive, non-discursive characteristics of musicality on the one hand and of animality on the other, have become invisible to us: another dimension of the early modern stage that we now have to make a special effort to recapture. Yet it's worth grasping that Bottom's mode of acting, announced with such a flourish, would have been immediately recognised by the first audience of *A Midsummer Night's Dream*, certainly as inept, but even more crucially as 'old-fashioned'. Far from being 'text-based', or confined by and to the written words of the play, as Hamlet's advice to the players insists, it responds actively to the text at almost every point, and indeed treats it as a series of stimuli that generate unprompted, improvised, trumpeted performance. In one sense, it's hardly 'acting' at all. If strict adherence to the words set down on the page, and a commitment to the impersonation of the character whose lines they record, is the first principle of that activity – as Hamlet demands – then Bottom is no actor. What he embodies is a much older practice already mentioned in the previous chapter. It is called 'playing'.[4]

The essence of playing lies in a symbiotic relationship with the audience neatly characterised by the metaphor of the trumpeter. Adjustable, responsive, shifting position to 'get an eccho', it's far more concerned to interact with the material reality of the spectator's world than to impersonate a different 'reality' on the stage. In order to operate, it needs constantly to elicit reaction so that it can acknowledge and reply to that with an unrehearsed flow of repartee, which itself invites and inspires further reaction, and so on. It will of course employ non-discursive, non-verbal modes of communication: musical and other sounds, winks, nods, grimaces, gestures. The result is an alertly responsive mode of performance of a sort that recalls the way the old 'music-hall' entertainers used to operate in Britain, or the way the stand-up comic currently functions.

In effect, this forms the basis of what Jean Alter has identified as the theatrical event's 'performant function', as opposed to its 'referential function'.[5] Our tendency to reduce a play to what it refers to, to what it has to say about the world outside itself, beyond the theatre's walls, is reinforced by our wholesale involvement in literacy and accentuated by our consequent commitment to 'text'. But, as Weimann incisively points out, that leaves aside a number of identifiable features that, reinforced by an early modern society's largely oral nature, typically surface in a play's permanent self-referring sense of performance and its lively awareness of its own existence in the theatre: elements so crucial that they could almost support a claim for the existence of 'performance' as an intransitive cultural practice and agency in its own right, unsustained by written documents. Deeply ingrained, the capacity, not to 'act' in the sense of 'imitate', but just to 'perform' *tout court* undoubtedly functioned as a crucial element in that society's whole way of life.[6]

The result, when it came to the staging of a play, was an investment in the kind of creative 'departure' from the text against which Hamlet and other playwrights (including Shakespeare) rail, but which we can now recognise as the vestigial remains of an older tradition that saw itself, rightly, in competition with a newer 'written' mode. One of the terms Weimann proposes for such inventive departures is 'disfigurement'; those stratagems whereby the player, ever trawling the audience for a fruitful response, may produce a special kind of 'deformative' effect by somehow adding to, interfering with, or 'bending' the text so that it begins to impart a different, perhaps almost contrary, sense to that which it overtly proposes.

Such deformation serves precisely to project the 'performance' beyond the text, and to propel it into a quite different realm. The ways in which jazz and other musicians will creatively 'deform' written-down musical notes, or sequences of chords, or even play their instruments 'wrongly' in order to produce unexpected, literally unheard-of, effects may offer an appropriate modern analogy. In fact, the process in the theatre was well understood and indeed recommended in the twentieth century by Bertolt Brecht, whose notion of 'alienation' it underpins and helps to define. In a 'non-aristotelian' theatre, such devices, Brecht argued, would enable an actor to 'stand outside' a character, much as a comedian does. By means of that kind of 'alienated' interaction with the audience, he or she would not 'become' the character, so much as enable themselves to step aside from it, and hand the part, and the issues at stake in its speeches, over to the audience.[7]

It is, as Weimann makes clear, just the sort of 'performing' that Peter Quince urges on Bottom and the other hempen homespuns:

one must come in with a bush of thorns and a lantern, and say he comes to disfigure or to present the person of Moonshine.

(3.1.56–7)

– a turn of phrase that underlines a commitment, less to impersonation, than to a 'presentation' of characters from the outside. In fact, the mechanicals' heavy-handed manipulation of dramatic conventions serves, in effect, to make manifest the complex nature of 'playing's relationship between performer and audience, player and part, and this, surely, is the serious point animating Bottom's famous injunction concerning the playing of the Lion. Its central requirements involve a deliberate disruption of the 'text', a stepping aside from one's part, a direct address to the audience, and the studied 'presentation' of one's role to them:

Nay, you must name his name, and half his face must be seen through the lion's neck; and he himself must speak through, saying thus, or to the same defect: 'Ladies', or 'Fair ladies, I would wish you,' or 'I would request you,' or 'I would entreat you, not to fear, not to tremble: my life for yours! If you think I come hither as a lion, it were pity of my life. No, I am no such thing; I am a man, as other men are': and there, indeed, let him name his name, and tell them plainly he is Snug the joiner.

(3.1.35ff.)

What Weimann terms the 'doubleness of the theatrical frame of reference', the simultaneous presence of the 'world-in-the-play' and 'play-in-the-world', of the represented and that which does the representing, is clearly in evidence here.[8] It's an explosive, propulsive conjunction.

Harry Harry

Of all Shakespeare's plays, *Henry V* is the one that most clearly explores and manipulates the early modern theatre's crucial duality. From the beginning, the chorus presumes, and draws specific attention to the play's dependence on, what S.L. Bethell described as the audience's 'double consciousness'[9]:

>   ... pardon, gentles all,
> The flat unraised spirits that hath dared
> On this unworthy scaffold to bring forth
> So great an object. Can this cockpit hold
> The vasty fields of France? Or may we cram
> Within this wooden O the very casques
> That did affright the air at Agincourt?
> O pardon, since a crooked figure may
> Attest in little place a million,
> And let us, ciphers to this great account,
> On your imaginary forces work.
> [...]
> Piece out our imperfections with your thoughts.
> Into a thousand parts divide one man
> And make imaginary puissance.
> Think, when we talk of horses, that you see them
> Printing their proud hoof i' th' receiving earth.
> For 'tis your thoughts that now must deck our kings...
>   (Prologue 8–28)

In effect, the gap probed here between the theatre's two spheres, the world of the play's narrative and the other, here-and-now world of the stage on which it is being played, furnishes the context in and, as Weimann suggests, generates the 'energy' on which 'playing' thrives. Its 'duplicity' creates, after all, the area where comedians and choruses have their being: it is what enables and promotes that stepping out of the story and in to the sort of direct interaction with the spectators in which Bottom deals, and it's significant that even 'so great an object' as the subject of *Henry V* is not considered too lofty for its employment.

In *A Midsummer Night's Dream*, the final alienating springboard from which the vault beyond the text is launched surely manifests itself in those moments when Bottom finds himself utterly 'disfigured' by his translation into an animal. But his alienated function has been foreshadowed from the first by his comic name, just as a wholesale commitment to 'playing' has been reinforced by the names of his fellow mechanicals and their relationship to the performance they so strenuously rehearse. Lower-class names in this play crudely sketch the social status and roles of their owners, so that whatever else the name Bottom achieves, it to some degree also systematically suppresses the sense of an individual, 'imitatable' person accessible by 'acting'. Naming, as we have seen, is precisely the stratagem by which an appropriately alienated Snug will be enabled to 'present' the Lion, rather than become identified with it. Yet it is in the strange combination of naming and animality that we sense the factor that seems decisively to fuel the ascent beyond the text.

We might presume that Bottom would have approved of what appears to be a related systematic 'naming' procedure in the second tetralogy of history plays. For in so far as they chronicle that most crucial of English projects, the generation of the massive ideological construct known as 'Great Britain', it's apparently a matter of some urgency that the name 'Henry' should be Anglicised and domesticated to 'Hal' at an early stage. By *Henry V*, the King is called 'Henry' only once (5.2.237). Instead, as when addressing his 'band of brothers' on St Crispin's day, he emphatically and dramatically signals another preference.

It is Harry. He is, he tells us, 'Harry the King'. And from then on, the battle-cry central to both play and political project proceeds effortlessly to fuse his name with his nationality in 'God for Harry, England and St. George' (3.1.34). Indeed, at a telling moment, the French King urges his ornately named knights against a figure whose name sounds, by comparison, wonderfully 'snug':

> High dukes, great princes, barons lords and knights,
> For your great seats now quit you of great shames.
> Bar Harry England that sweeps through our land...
> (3.5.46–8)

Yet it's more than simply cosy: this is also an explosive, propulsive moment. For if we look closely at the blood-stained figure who confronts us here, and if we link with 'Harry England' the emblem of the 'warlike Harry' that the Chorus describes at the beginning of the play, with his three snarling dogs, named Famine, Sword and Fire who 'Crouch for employment' at his side, we begin to discern a familiar animal figure. It forces us to confront a serious question. If to give a bear the name 'Harry' undoubtedly lends it a disturbing power in the bear-baiting arena, what happens in the theatre next door, when you give the same name to a King?

The sense of suddenly soaring beyond the words on the page is powerful. Yet an attempt to address that question more precisely surely fails. It is to try self-consciously to step inside the cultural world that an early modern theatre-goer unreflectingly inhabits. To find oneself finally unable to answer it is to recognise that the contours of our own world are crucially different from theirs. The gap between them remains, however much we delude ourselves, virtually unbridgeable. Some connection between naming and animality is observably at stake, and the conjunction is evidently an explosive, if ineffable, one, opening up a 'playing' dimension far beyond the controlling limits of textuality. It's a tantalising prospect, but finally ungraspable and unmanageable in any material detail. Whatever names seem to whisper, history always deafens us.

Of course, all proper names confidently propose and invest in a sense of unified subjectivity; a personal coherence apparently able to withstand the dissipating onrush of time. As 'texts', names seek to fix and contain human beings. Time, however, usually blows that gaff. Monarchs' names are particularly false friends. King Henry V's first pronouncements on succeeding to the throne make it very clear that the transfer of his personal diminutive to his predecessor is a matter of distinctive national policy:

> This is the English, not the Turkish court;
> Not Amurath an Amurath succeeds,
> But Harry Harry.
>
> (*2 Henry IV*, 5.2.47–9)

But we know that, in truth, Henry V will not be remotely the same as Henry IV, any more than an essential likeness links Henry VII and Henry VI.[10] That onward, numbered march hints at a capacity for repetition that can acknowledge, engage with and finally defeat change, but it works, as a matter of politics, only to conceal it. In the end, the whiff of sameness that succession brings will always be dispelled by its final decline into difference. 'The King is dead, long live the King' is merely a centuries-long whistling in the dark, and wish-fulfilment as much as exasperation surely invests Henry VIII's motto *Eadem*

Semper. If history has a single lesson, it can only be that nothing is, or ever can be, 'always the same'.

That unresolvable opposition of permanence and mutability, timelessness and history, gnaws at the heart of any monarchical culture, burrowing ruinously beneath its first political principle, infiltrating all of its discursive practices. Naturally, it inhabits some of the major themes of Shakespeare's plays and it's hardly surprising to discover it deeply embedded in everything he wrote. The Bard was always wary even of regularising his own name by the imposition on it of a single, unifying sameness. *Eadem Semper* may be fine for kings, but Shakespeare's father used sixteen different ways of spelling the family name and the playwright at least five. Even in his will, Shakespeare's name appears with two spellings.

But nobody knows the answer to the question posed above principally because it's a query directed to the past, and we can't step outside the present in order to ask, let alone answer it. On the other hand, when a presentist criticism considers the question of a strategy that might be adequate to the demands of these plays, the abandonment of some sort of historicising project seems at first to commit us to a far more daunting possibility: a myth of transcendence in support of the sentimental fiction that they have a capacity somehow to float free of their contexts, to embrace a mysteriously 'universal' human experience and with it the consolations of a no less mysterious trans-historical and trans-cultural 'human nature'. It is certainly the case that too much teaching of Shakespeare is devoted nowadays to the kind of simple-minded 'sameness' (how like us the Elizabethans were), that ignores history. Too little concerns itself with the analysis of 'difference' (how unlike us the Elizabethans were), which requires some serious grappling with it. These are not mutually exclusive poles, but criticism is surely more profitably employed when it inclines towards the second, which demands a certain degree of conceptual rigour, than the first, which produces the kind of vacuous cheer-leading that, for example, Harold Bloom (no Harry he) has sought to dignify as the 'awe' we owe Stratford's 'mortal god'.[11]

On balance, it seems better to face up to the fact – recognised as a first principle by any self-respecting presentism – that the questions we ask of a literary text will always be shaped by our own concerns. To embrace that is not to abandon the past.

In fact, perhaps it offers the makings of a subtler engagement with it: one that both promotes and probes the suggestion, to paraphrase the historian E.H. Carr, that there are few more significant pointers to the character of any society than the kind of Shakespearean criticism it writes, or fails to write.[12]

ABC

> our analysis, which has hitherto been qualitative, must become quantitative; we must cease to be empirical and become scientific; in criticism as in other matters, the test that decides between science and empiricism is this: 'Can you say, not only of what kind, but how much? If you cannot weigh, measure, number your results, however you may be convinced yourself, you must not hope to convince others . . . you are merely a guesser'.[13]

Thus the Shakespearean critic the Reverend Frederick G. Fleay, unsurprisingly nicknamed 'the industrious flea'. The occasion was the inaugural meeting, in 1874, of a new society devoted to the study of the Bard. Its founder had deliberately made a point of locating it and its activities firmly 'in this Victorian time, when our geniuses of Science are so wresting her secrets from nature as to make our days memorable forever' and he was certainly himself one of that time's most remarkable products.[14] Educated at University College, London, and Cambridge University, Frederick James Furnivall (1825–1910) was a barrister, a supporter of Trade Unionism and a model Christian Socialist, helping to found one of the original Working Men's Colleges.[15]

Energy of that order needs diverse outlets and Furnivall soon abandoned the law to embark on the massive series of learned projects that guarantee him a place in any history of the academic study of English Literature. A great believer in accurate textual scholarship, he founded the Early English Text Society in 1864 and later went on to found the Browning Society and the Shelley Society. In 1873, he founded what was to be possibly the most contentious of his enterprises: the New Shakspere Society.

The Society's objects can stand as the very model of Victorian scientism.[16] Its central project was nothing less than Darwinian: 'The subject of growth, the oneness of Shakespeare, the links between his successive plays, the distinctive characteristics of each period and its contrast with the others, the treatment of the same or like incidents etc. in the different periods of Shakspere's life'.[17] In fact, the honorary Presidency of the Society was initially offered to Darwin, who wisely declined. The aim, none the less, remained crudely 'scientific', resolutely 'textual': to pin Shakespeare and his words down, once and for all: to get his life and times straight, his plays accurately edited and classified, to align the one exactly with the other, to fix the shape of both irretrievably, and to weld them together for ever as a single, comprehensible and coherent unity. Any suggestion of duplicitous repartee, or extra-textual, non-discursive 'playing' interchange with the audience clearly had little place in the weighing, measuring, numbering world traversed by the industrious flea.

In pursuit of these goals, Furnivall's description of himself as a kind of 'scientific botanist'[18] proved accurate enough, for the Society fostered and relied on what he didn't hesitate to call 'that most powerful and useful instrument in Shakspere criticism', the Metrical Test.[19] Metrical Tests, the special interest of the Reverend Fleay, purported to be 'scientific' accounts of the various prosodic and rhythmic arrangements within Shakespeare's lines. They would, both Furnivall and the flea believed, determine the sequence in which the plays were composed, so that the critic would then be able to 'use that revised order for the purpose of studying the progress and meaning of Shakespeare's mind, the passage of it from the fun and word-play, the lightness, the passion, of the Comedies of Youth, through the patriotism ... of the Histories of Middle Age, to the great Tragedies dealing with the deepest questions of man in Later Life ... etc'.[20]

The coherence and unity apparently offered by names couldn't help but prove attractive in such a context and something of the rigour with which Furnivall pursued his quarry can be judged from his insistence on a particular spelling of the Bard's name: 'Shakspere'. Claiming that, scientifically, if not botanically, analysed, the signatures all read the same, he concluded that '...though it has hitherto been too much to ask people to suppose that Shakspere knew how to spell his own name, I hope the demand may not prove too great for the

imagination of the members of the New Shakspere Society'.[21]
The demands turned out to be too great for others, however,
and a certain amount of derision directed at Furnivall's scientism proved inevitable. Equally inevitably, since nomenclature
is ever the false friend of those in pursuit of rigour, it focused
precisely on names. In 1876, John Jeremiah anonymously published *Furnivallos Furioso and The Newest Shakespeare Society*, a
poorly rhymed satirical sketch, which featured an egregious
and overexcited Leader claiming

> I'll found a fresh Society, call'd 'New'
> And try if I can't, by much reading hard
> Impart 'new readings' to th' 'Immortal Bard'[22]

In the same year the poet Swinburne wrote a piece arguing that
Shakespeare was the sole author of the play *Henry VIII*. Furnivall, botanist's antennae aquiver, was quick to point out errors
in the case. Swinburne protested. A row then gradually spread
itself across several journals, degenerating quickly into mali-
cious, personal abuse. Evidently feeling that his own intuitive
critical capacities were more trustworthy than any system of
pseudo-scientific analysis, Swinburne began to refer acidly to
'the duncery and quackery of a Sham Shakespeare Society'.
Furnivall responded that the intuitive organ in question, Swinburne's ear, was merely 'a poetaster's, hairy, thick and dull'.

Further salvoes quickly ensued, and a whiff of playing's rib-
aldry quickly starts to rise from beneath the New Shakspere
Society's tightly clamped lid. Names were its primary vehicle,
and it's interesting to note that, as the temperature rises and an
unruly ripple of repartee (the very stuff of an outlawed
'playing') begins to splash the measured prose of 'scientific'
scholarship, a certain animality (already lurking in the sobriquet of the Reverend Fleay) invests them to boot. Furnivall
began to send postcards to Swinburne's friends in which he
fetchingly underlined the hirsute quality of the poet's aural
equipment by renaming him 'Pigsbrook' (a bit of spoof lexico-
graphy in which 'Swin' equates with 'pig' and 'burne' with
'brook'). Swinburne's riposte, scarcely rapier-like, was to name
Furnivall 'Brotheldyke' (on the same principle: combining the
Latin 'fornix' and 'vallum'). The two of them then proceeded
to engage in a self-destructive flyting match that might have

been the envy of any early modern comedian. Its lowest ebb was plumbed when, giving nomenclature its full 'playing' rein, Swinburne began to refer to Furnivall as 'Fartiwell' and the Society as 'The Shitspeare Society'.[23] *Nomen est omen* perhaps. In this case, execration was certainly followed by evacuation. Friends fled, Bardolaters bolted, membership declined and the Society eventually closed.

Several years later, voicing a grand dismay at the perceivable decline of a more heroic world than the present, the poet T.S. Eliot posed the mysteriously evocative question 'Where are the eagles and the trumpets?' ('A Cooking Egg', 1919). Even though the reference clearly glances at Shakespeare's *Coriolanus*, it has the broad allusive fall-out of major poetry, despite Eliot's own characteristic, even Coriolanus-like, hauteur. Eagles and trumpets, ancient sound and spectacle, the stuff, not just of the Roman imperium, but of the early modern stage that Eliot so admired, no longer have significance in the reduced twentieth-century world. Where are they indeed? Eliot's wry answer to that question hits a vital cultural target. The absurdities of the weighing, the measuring, the numbering, even the spelling of a Furnivallesque textuality in full fig can stand as apt symbols of Coriolanus's and Shakespeare's decline. In our dumbed-down 'penny world', a vital oral art dwindles into a series of dry-as-dust, regularised 'scientific' editions. The extent of the depletion is suggested by the image of a degraded populace mournfully ingesting its paltry, processed diet in the (to Eliot) disastrous democracy of a well-known chain of tea-shops. The hint of a restricting abcedary regime in the initials of their proprietors, the Aerated Bread Company, makes the answer to the question 'Where are the eagles and the trumpets?' as scathing as it is patronising:

> Buried beneath some snow-deep Alps.
> Over buttered scones and crumpets
> Weeping, weeping multitudes
> Droop in a hundred A.B.C.'s.
> ('A Cooking Egg' ll. 30–3)

Rat

Does Victorian 'scientific' textuality deserve a better monument? A year after Furnivall's death, a memorial volume of reminiscences was careful to record his habit of holding court in the ABC teashop on the first floor of 66 New Oxford Street. It went so far as to include – as a tribute to his liberal principles – a brief piece by one of the waitresses there who particularly remembered him.[24] Her name was Blanche Huckle. The playful, almost Shakespearean echo of that – to say nothing of its potential as a vehicle for Eliotic scorn – follows Furnivall to his grave. Yet it was only part of a larger pattern of nominal harrying. Years after the closure of the New Shakspere Society, on a visit to the Reading Room in The British Museum, Swinburne barely noticed a venerable old man who lifted his head as he passed. On hearing subsequently that it was Furnivall, he exclaimed – name-calling to the last – 'Tiens! Was that the dog?'[25]

The casual surfacing of animality will not by now surprise us. But Pigsbrook could just as readily have saluted Brotheldyke in another, no less zoological, mode. For a number of years the author Kenneth Grahame had acted as the Honorary Secretary of the New Shakspere Society, and it's perhaps fitting that Furnivall's ultimate destiny was to serve as the model for the character of the Rat in his *The Wind in the Willows*. Strangely, that final, winsome, immortalising touch might serve to place him even more decisively than his scheme for settling the Bard's historical hash. Is it possible that 'Ratty' and his friends, with their quaint public-school slang, their cosy plying of hamper, toast and teapot, their unhesitating contempt for the poorly spoken, property-invading, red-eyed scavengers, the weasels, might offer a useful purchase on the essence of New Shakspere-ism? Are they the lighter side of a cruder project whereby Shakespeare's cruel and savage England itself contracts into a kind of comfy theme park, thronged by the outrageous and endearing, but surrounded by a wild wood peopled by foreign weasely creatures? Is a clanking, blinkered nuts-and-bolts textualism, resolutely pinning down, classifying and measuring, merely the other side of a depoliticising, infantilising project whose uncomplicated notions of universality deliberately reduce society to the interplay of loveable, hissable or, worse, endlessly discussable 'characters'?

That for years the Royal Shakespeare Theatre at Stratford put on annual, and hugely successful, dramatisations of *The Wind in the Willows* is only one of the ironies generated by the massive expansion in the nineteenth and twentieth centuries of the Bard's role as an instrument for educating the young. Grahame's book (dramatised by A.A. Milne) becomes in this context the confirming 'holiday' fare of a regime whose more usual workaday commitment turns what was once popular art into the arbiter of intelligence, civility and learning. It would surely have astonished Shakespeare to find the hierarchies ordained by modern economic structures reinforced by his plays in their guise as linchpin of the academic subject called 'English'.

It would also be misleading to present the English language as a world-wide tyranny. Yet millions of English-speakers whose speech signals their own subjugation in one or another of those hierarchies will be well acquainted with the disruptive energies such a system can release. The spectrum is a broad one. Systematically deprived of a native discourse in some cases, incarcerated by a degrading accent in others, they live bound to an oppressor's tongue but with no guaranteed share in its bounty; forced into mimicry, or required to engage the contours of one way of life in modes and with names that remain ignominiously shackled to another. In the inevitable struggle for ownership of the means of signification that such a situation breeds, parallel but distinct orders of meaning often come to inhabit the same linguistic structures, and when these compete, the stakes will inevitably be high. We have become familiar with the day-to-day resort of underclasses to slang, patois, and deliberately mystifying words and phrases. At the heart of all subversive rhetorical practice in which a subordinate culture invades and refashions the products of its dominant partner, particularly the individual words or names of the language it is forced to share, there lies a revolutionary principle of revision, of rebellious renaming, of the letting of cats out of linguistic bags. To vault the fences of nomination and signification is always, as the anarchic, poop-pooping Toad knew, to challenge what counts as reality.

Sweet thunder

In addition to its other distinctions, the last year of the previous millennium marked the hundredth anniversary of the birth of one of the great artists of the twentieth century. Born in the USA, in Washington, DC, his name was Edward Kennedy Ellington. As a black speaker of English, Ellington inherited a keen sense of language's, and particularly of naming's, subversive, 'playing', refashioning potential. After all, the lady who taught him the piano was called Mrs Klinkscales. And in adopting, at a very early stage, the sobriquet 'Duke' he was, of course, drawing on precisely that black American tradition of naming in which the desire for validation often runs in tandem with the urge to undercut the social hierarchy that controls it.

In 1956, Duke Ellington and his orchestra were invited to play at the Shakespeare Festival in Stratford, Ontario. As a result, he embarked on the composition of a new suite first performed in its entirety in New York Town Hall on 28 April 1957. Devoted to Shakespearean themes, its name returns us to those lines from *A Midsummer Night's Dream* with which this chapter began. He called it *Such Sweet Thunder*. It's probably an oversimplification to suggest that Ellington's sense of the occasion prompted him to present his music and his musicians as a quasi-savage, animal-like intrusion into the aesthetic niceties of mid-century Shakespearean production (although the orchestra's lead trumpeter at this time was named 'Cat' Anderson). Nevertheless, the notion of *concordia discors* captures perfectly the essence of its remarkable achievement as 'sweet thunder', with its trumpets effortlessly taking up that older sense of 'playing', exploding with reckless, non-discursive immediacy to find 'ecchoes' that embrace and involve an astonished and delighted audience. William Tawyer would have been proud of them.

It's been suggested many times that black music, such as jazz, with its commitment to the improvised re-working of the chord structure of original melodies, has always represented a major American challenge to the European idea of an author's or composer's (or, *mutatis mutandis*, a king's) authority, unity and coherence.[26] Far from being parasitic on or limited to the service of the author's or composer's art, its function, as Geoffrey Hartman has argued, is creative, its relationship with

its object symbiotic, interpretative, constitutive. To add the
term 'critical' to that list is merely to underline the claim that
the same range of principles characterises the non-servile practice of an appropriate literary response.[27]

Certainly, the value to us of Ellington's genuinely American
'reading' of Shakespeare lies in what might be called the presentist, 'playing' stance it playfully but significantly adopts,
particularly in the case of the piece devoted to *Henry V*. This is
called 'Sonnet to *Hank Cinq*', and here the name clearly is the
game. Its racy irreverence in the face of the serried ranks of
British monarchy marks it as firmly republican. Its determined
pulling of the name Henry – not into a distilled Englishness, as
'Harry' does, but across the Atlantic, with 'Hank' marks it
equally firmly as American. Even more American is its allegiance in the matter of something so fundamental as numbering. To fight free of Englishness by turning to things French
has, after all, been a major transatlantic ploy from the eight-
eenth century. That '*Hank Cinq*' does all this whilst overtly presenting itself as simply submitting to the rigours of assonance
reinforces a sense of joky subversion.

Whether it has any claim to speak for, even to represent, a
new approach to the Bard is difficult to say. The extent to
which it underwrites or helps us recognise and come to terms
with whatever figure might be dimly seen gesturing at us
through this book's semantic grid can hardly be clear. But at
the very least, music's quintessential, non-discursive nature
immediately projects *Hank Cinq* beyond the reach of one kind
of textuality, just as jazz music's ultimate independence of any
'written' requirement makes performativity so fundamental a
factor that the early modern distinction between 'playing' and
'acting' seems crucially at stake here. Is it too outrageous to
propose a reading of history in which the textually based
demands of the latter have gradually, as part of the development of a particular social and economic formation, obscured
the older, no less insistent, dimensions of the former? Is it
absurdly reductionist to suggest that a determined suppression
of the uncertainties of the 'playing' dimension of drama is evidently part and parcel of that enterprise: that this is how one
sort of social and economic structure works, through the construction of an objectified, weighable and measurable world,
manageable by the instrumental reason of its inhabitants – a

world permanently and precisely captured in, fixed and regulated by, a specific notion and use of texts? Certainly, by the end of the nineteenth century, whatever the socialist credentials of its proponents, any 'New Shakspere' would be required to test all its claims for cultural authority against the integrity of the text it both served and had materially helped to produce. It follows that the challenge from the left for any post-capitalist criticism will surely lie in the proposal that, at work underneath that surface, there was always – and there remains – a just-discernible, non-textual, perhaps non-discursive and even non-human dimension, which requires fully to be confronted in the twenty-first century.

As I've tried to suggest above, it tends to burst through in terms of names. But if names are tiny 'texts' with which we seek to pin down and permanently fix human beings, they are also words, and thus part of language, and they partake inevitably of language's 'playing' dimension, its ultimate indeterminacy. What threatens to erupt in them is something that fundamentally challenges the notion of the human they – and perhaps language at large – seek to enclose. It is that 'rough beast', currently slouching towards the academy to be born, that presents us with a major and disconcerting critical challenge whose implications stretch well beyond those usually associated with the Bard.

What will it look like? Of course, it won't be a bear, and it's name won't be Harry. It'll be shadowy no doubt, but perhaps less compelling than shifty and inconclusive. Its arguments won't really seem to hang together. The connections it proposes will seem arch, tenuous, linked, if at all, in some rhapsodic, jazzy way that owes scandalously little to the procedures of traditional text-based scholarship. In fact, if it reminds us of anything, it's most likely to be a band of dilapidated, self-conscious, repartee-wielding performers, preceded by an anonymous colleague who's about to raise a trumpet to his lips. The first task is of course to recognise that instrument's existence, then its potential, and to discern the challenge it implies. The least we can do is to respond to its propulsive call, trusting that the performance will finally project us into 'the concord of this discord'. Both Dukes, Ellington no less than Theseus, seem to recommend that as the real, the only way to travel. O bliss! O poop-poop!

8

Conclusion: Speaking to You in English

Obiter dictum

'This is Terence Hawkes, speaking to you in English.' Barely permissible at the beginning of a book, such words are probably no more defensible at its end. So let me hasten to add that their purpose is commemoration rather than condescension. The phrase aims deliberately to recall one of the great, mysterious figures of the British music-hall and of radio: a comedian named Gillie Potter.

On stage, Potter always wore a faded blue blazer and a straw hat. His act consisted quite simply of a monologue, solemnly delivered in a clipped, relentlessly cut-glass accent, deliberately reminiscent of the BBC news-readers of the 1930s. It always began – in a parody of BBC technique – with the words 'This is Gillie Potter, speaking to you in English'. It was meant to be funny, to British audiences of my generation and older it was extremely funny, and that phrase was the key to it. Its absurd, insistent repetition, its bland deployment of the sublimely superfluous, was crucial. Somehow, its utter redundancy managed to produce a comic *hauteur* as endearing to its audience as it was infantilising. The fact that English is a widely spoken language was part of the joke. Of course, a sharper political edge might just have emerged if that were not the native language of those whom Potter addressed: that is, in the sort of colonial setting at which his dress and slightly languid manner hinted. Its full potential becomes evident more or less at the moment when he thrived: the period before and during the Second World War, when the British Empire, like his blazer and himself, faded and finally failed.

Gillie Potter's self-presentation, his manner, his straw boater, his exquisite superfluity, focus attention on a major paradox: that of the individual who, for all his eccentric singularity, nevertheless 'stands for', and thus consistently repeats, something much larger than himself: in this case, nothing less than England. For there was no doubt that on stage – twice nightly – Potter represented the kind of 'Englishness' that the between-wars English happily embraced, or wanted to embody. Language, and the way it is used, has come to be one of the main instruments of political power in our time. Overtly self-mocking, but covertly self-confident, Gillie Potter's use of English offers a telling example of it in action. He made a profession out of what might be called a radically English stance: power masquerading as a kind of dotty weakness, pride backing wryly into a lime-lit humility, success dutifully donning the lineaments of failure. Indeed, failure was meat and drink to Potter. He failed to conform to the popular idea of a comedian. His mock objectivity notably failed to control the anarchic behaviour of the characters he invented, and their own personal failures were the very stuff of his chronicles. He even made much of the fact that he had failed his final examinations at Oxford. In short, he was a supremely successful failure whose authority derived entirely from his use of language. No wonder we were putty – or clay – in his hands.

With a batty, dilapidated Englishness as his target, the fictional village Potter reported on bore the quintessentially English name of 'Hogsnorton', and he styled himself its Sage. One of its most memorable characters gloried in the absurdly English title of 'Lord Marshmallow' and a supremely English painter was regularly invoked in the famous pair of paintings said to grace the walls of Hogsnorton Manor: 'Lord Marshmallow after Constable', and its matching masterpiece, 'Constable after Lord Marshmallow'. Nevertheless, the dour defence of a way of life and of its concomitant privileges that peeps from under this joky façade confirms something that people outside England have always known: 'speaking to you in English' is a political act.

Sceptred isles

Along with Gillie Potter, the other major icon of Englishness for my generation was the balding glassy-eyed figure whose mere outline on banknotes and credit cards signals that he also stands for a particular way of life. I refer of course to Shakespeare. The way his work is currently (and in my view, wrongly) taught in our schools, it often seems to offer a kind of hymn to hearty English individualism. Accordingly, the plays end up as little more than portrait galleries of quirky 'characters' who love, hate, but mostly – word beloved of examiners – 'develop'. How fitting, the unstated – or all too often stated – thesis goes, that this collection of singular, well-defined individuals should spring from the pen of the national poet of the 'island race': a Gillie Potter in doublet and hose.

In fact, the same sense of singularity, of self-sufficiency, of clear-cut and well-defined boundaries, links both individualism and the nationalism it paradoxically serves. Thus one kind of 'Englishness' merges readily enough with a Hogsnortoned notion of England as a ring-fenced, clearly marked, independent and walled-off area of the sort famously described by John of Gaunt in *Richard II*:

> This royal throne of kings, this sceptr'd isle,
> This earth of majesty, this seat of Mars,
> This other Eden, demi-paradise,
> This fortress built by Nature for herself
> Against infection and the hand of war,
> This happy breed of men, this little world,
> This precious stone set in the silver sea,
> Which serves it in the office of a wall,
> Or as a moat defensive to a house
> Against the envy of less happier lands,
> This blessèd plot, this earth, this realm, this England . . .
>
> (*Richard II*, 2.1.40–50)

Like any semiotic practice, poetic description is inevitably involved, beyond its referential targets, in the discourses that weave the fabric of a national culture. In this case, a glance at the map confirms what geography has materially decreed. England is not, never has been and, unless some cataclysm intervenes, never will be an island encircled by the sea. In short, the 'sceptr'd isle' is as much an invention as the 'English-ness' for which the plays at large are said effectively to speak.

Maybe, as servants of ideologies, Bards have a licence to sub-edit whatever mere nature proposes. Yet it's odd to find such an obviously misleading account of the physical world repeat-edly presented and rehearsed as proper, desirable, even 'natural', across four hundred years, latterly by teachers of the academic subject of which Shakespeare is the linchpin. Thus, an essay by G. Wilson Knight, one of the most influential Shakespearean critics of the mid-twentieth century, opens with these astonishing remarks:

> England is an island. Though that is surely obvious enough, we do not always remember it, nor all that it implies. By it our history has been moulded.

Of course, Knight was writing at a time of crisis. The essay in question is the text of a lecture given in London in 1940 and published as a pamphlet not inappropriately titled *This Sceptred Isle: Shakespeare's Message for England at War* (Knight, 1940). Throughout it, 'England' appears as the sole signifier for Britain, whilst the divine plan for the 'sovereign part to be played' by the English-speaking nations 'in establishment of world-justice, world-order, and world-peace' is solemnly, not to say chillingly rehearsed.[1] Echoing across the length and breadth of Shakespeare's plays, Knight argues, we can hear the 'voice of England', moving inexorably to distil, in Cranmer's prophecy in *Henry VIII*, the Bard's 'message' for us; its animat-ing 'island' notion reinforced, if not exactly licensed, by Queen Elizabeth I's prayer before her navy's victory over the Armada:

> O! let thine enemies know that thou hast received England, which they most of all for thy Gospel's sake do malign, into thine own protection. Set a wall about it, O Lord, and evermore mightily defend it.[2]

Flying in the face of fact, geographical fact at that, is a practice perhaps sanctioned to some extent by the exigencies of war and the need, in 1940 no less than in earlier times, to stiffen the sinews and summon up the blood. That might excuse Knight's slightly tetchy tone: it might even help to mitigate the bravado of 'that is surely obvious enough'. But assertions concerning the moulding of our history are perhaps more troubling. Here they serve to demonstrate that nature remains ever culture's creature and that the chimerical island of 'England after Gaunt' shares sufficient ideological baggage with the fanciful painting 'Lord Marshmallow after Constable' to make the point. To use the terms developed in previous chapters, it's evident that, in 1940, Knight's Shakespearean criticism readily assumed a 'presentist' stance, whereby the then current European upheavals became the basis for a powerful and influential analysis of the plays.

Double or nothing

Perhaps part of its power derived from its apparently effortless engagement with some of the deep-lying structures that lurk within the British national psyche. A sense of barricaded insularity and a commitment to the consoling recitation of past triumphs connects smoothly enough with the backward-looking name of the conflict in question. For however loudly it may be proclaimed as the beginning of a new age, the 'Second' World War inevitably presents itself in terms of its own subsequence, its fundamental nature as a 'repeat'.

It's a styling whose own presentist thrust forces us to reread the past in its image, and requires the nomination of the events of 1914–18 as 'First', or as 'World War I', to its 'Second'. As a result, the numerical designation, 'World War II', has come to seem more and more appropriate in an atmosphere in which World War III has occasionally seemed a possibility, and in which the massive horrors of World War I might to some degree be slightly mitigated by their status, not as unique, but as the first in a manageable series. Certainly the 'Second' World War's wholesale revisionary deployment of copies, replicas, fakes, camouflage – even the development by British intelligence of a 'Double Cross' system for second-guessing enemy agents – seems oddly to confirm this aspect of its modernity.

Perhaps it's true that we now belong, as Hillel Schwartz has suggested, to a 'culture of the copy' in which an overt admiration for originality, authenticity, the one-off, finds itself systematically undermined by a covert and more powerful commitment to reproduction, duplication, and the facsimile. As he concludes, we may profess to admire the unique, but our first response is usually to try to reproduce it.[3] To the extent that a copy presupposes an 'original', or that a simulacrum presupposes a preceding 'genuine article', these concepts work to convince us of the existence of a primary, grounded sphere prior to the secondary 'reel' world of recorded and replayable sound and vision. In the process, they serve ultimately to bolster nostalgia for a lost Eden of singularity, a vanished demi-Paradise of unified and coherent self-presence, an island 'England' forever set in a silver sea.

The second chapter of this book has already dealt at some length with the matter of repetition. If our habits of recapitulation, simulation, copying operate so crucially to make existence meaningful for us, then, at the very least, this requires a revaluation of them as strategies for reaching the truth. It's a tricky business, because although 'repeats' apparently refer, straightforwardly enough, beyond themselves, it's not clear that they can ever guarantee wholly unmediated access to what precedes them. Football fans, savants of the slow-motion television replay, know how easily that device can generate narratives quite different from those sworn to by eyewitnesses or confirmed by officials. Newly conscripted subscribers to the principle that you can't tell the same story twice, they share the same radical perception with Jorge Luis Borges's Pierre Menard, the ineffable 'author of *Don Quixote*'. As Borges mischievously says of his principled plagiarist, 'The text of Cervantes and that of Menard are verbally identical, but the second is almost infinitely richer'.[4] He's right. In theory, repetition, simulation, copying may be the midwives of sameness. In practice, they tend the subtle womb of difference.

Kierkegaard puts the case bluntly: 'The dialectic of repetition is easy, for that which is repeated has been – otherwise it could not have been repeated – but the very fact that it has been makes the repetition into something new'.[5] Not only is a 'copy' always and everywhere something quite novel, different from that which has been copied, but repetition, or the genera-

tion of more of the same, systematically becomes less a stratagem for avoiding change, than the very basis of it: the key to
the construction of difference. And that involvement in difference makes repetition part of the construction of meaning.

The trouble is that our current view of the world tends to
leave difference out in the cold. As Gilles Deleuze points out,
our culture posits recognition of sameness as the dominant
mode of our thinking and tends to insist on that as its proper
goal. A strategy dedicated in general terms to the establishment
of this as the same as that ruthlessly subordinates difference to
identity, awarding it a prominence which then 'defines the
world of representation'.[6] We abhor contradiction and endorse
'likeness' – the recognition that this 'equals' that – as a fundamental indicator of 'truth'. At an unsophisticated level we even
like to think that this is how language works in relation to the
world; that words somehow 'equal' or repeat what they refer to;
that 'tree', say, has a tree-like quality that encourages and
underwrites the connection. We look for unified coherent
islands and we find them. The same strategy also presupposes
unity and coherence in the perceiver and thus serves to confirm
the prejudices that finally crystallise in that islander's credo:
cogito ergo sum. In our culture, identity and its cohorts, similarity,
resemblance, likeness, not only rule, they make the rules.

But if, for the moment, we turn this prejudice on its head
and, as Deleuze urges, 'think difference', everything changes.
Since there can be no immaculate 'sameness', there can be no
absolute repetition. Whatever returns affirms and confirms, by
returning, its difference. However carefully crafted, copies only
gesture towards an identity they cannot possibly realise. By that
very fact, and at the same time, they covertly insist upon and
silently reinforce the very distinctiveness and disparity that they
overtly deny. If there is no absolute repetition, there exist only
and everywhere degrees of difference. Seen thus, difference
becomes central to experience and a culture of the copy must
by the same token also be a culture deeply involved in the complexities of disparity. Clearly, a lot depends on how we choose
to read the material that confronts us.

Our way of life's preference in the matter may well be to
read for sameness. But linguistic meaning can most certainly be
said to derive, whether we like it or not, from an inward-
looking system, which proposes no equations with anything

beyond itself, and in which the differences between words operate as the central, determining feature. In the event, difference can never finally be ironed out of any aspect of our culture. It skulks, disconcertingly, at the heart of the most punctilious copy, much as, as we have seen Freud argue above, the discomfiting, uncanny *unheimlich* lurks at the centre of the domesticated, reassuring *heimlich*, coming to light, through repetition, as 'something repressed which recurs'.

Repetition's concealed investment in difference can thus only be neglected, never neutralised. That is what makes possible those disturbing, disjunctive 'leaps' beyond the straight and narrow paths of logic at which *Das Unheimliche* so penetratingly glances. Perceptible only out of the corner of the cultural eye, repetition's inherent capacity for the sudden, unnerving derailment of 'the same' shares a covert, 'unofficial' status with matters such as gesture, or 'tone of voice', those inevitable concomitants of speech between human beings which, although necessary, nevertheless embody a scandalous potential for undermining – or ironising – the overt 'meaning' of any utterance. The difference festering unappeased at the copy's centre enables it to tap into a similar resource: a cache of 'uncanny' energy capable of projecting it into a realm of implication beyond the discursive reach of language, or that predominantly verbal aspect of it which Hamlet contemptuously dismisses as 'words, words, words'.

What would a differently constituted culture, one which took that dimension fully into account, look like? One of the major readjustments required might well involve the promotion of a range of apparently second-order forms of communication, such as gesture, posture, dress, style, tone of voice, accent, manner, 'way of speaking', to a parity with logic, awarding them a licence to challenge the orthodoxies words draw on to sustain a narrow notion of 'sense'. These aspects of language would no longer appear accidental; mere excrescences, nuisances, decorations, or distractions. On the contrary, they would inherit an ancient relevance as elements of an immemorial world in which the non-discursive claims as much attention as the discursive, and from which the structures of thought encoded in superstition, contradiction, customs, riddles, jokes, foolishness and 'playing' have not yet been banished: a world in which, as in the case of bear-baiting, a non-logical, nonrational lore stands up to and challenges the logical, rationally codified equivalencies we enshrine in law. Its central art-form would be one that draws as much on non-verbal modes of communication, and on the massively generative powers of repetition, as on words. Shakespeare stands as the major exponent of this sort of art in English.

Play and replay

Thus *Hamlet*, it hardly needs saying, begins without words: not with the line, 'Who's there?' (1.1.1), but with Francisco's silent entry on to the stage, followed by that of Barnardo. The play ends without words too, as if to underline its potential independence of them. And in between, shadowing the speeches, yet never openly articulated, a huge, barely sounded dimension gradually looms, bringing hints of an extremely disturbing instance of 'repetition': the dawning possibility – it's no more than that – that Claudius may turn out to be Hamlet's father. The potential complications of that stalk the action almost from the first, and although the play says nothing overt on the matter, they persist, structurally implicit in and smouldering at the very heart of a situation in which a husband is murdered by his wife's lover.

Claudius's initial reference to Hamlet, 'But now, my cousin Hamlet, and my son', is only the first of a number of nudges from that quarter, just as Hamlet's immediate response, 'A little more than kin, and less than kind' (1.2.64–5), also worries obliquely at the issue. Most critics will counter that when Claudius says 'son', he means 'stepson'. Yet 'son' is what he says, and in a period when kings, for obvious reasons, had to be highly scrupulous in the matter of public acknowledgement of their children (Elizabeth's own legitimacy had been a matter of considerable concern) then the new King's use of this term might reasonably be said to give us pause. In performance, a barely audible intake of breath from the assembled courtiers, even a moment of stunned silence, is all that would be needed to set the play on fire.

The suggestion is emphatically not that Claudius is Hamlet's 'real' father. The play does not deal in that kind of verisimilitude, and its characters can claim no actual material existence outside it. No appeal is possible to a world beyond the theatre.

Within it, however, more felt than seen or heard, the issue remains none the less palpable: sensed underneath the narrative, always available through it – one effect, perhaps, of a sense of 'playing' that ranges well beyond the text on the page – it mocks at the events of the story as they unfold. Confirming hints of its presence multiply as the death of fathers begins to emerge more and more as a feature of the action. Claudius himself initiates what he stresses as a 'common theme':

> But you must know, your father lost a father,
> That father lost, lost his...
>
> (1.2.89–90)

So common is it that by the middle of the play attention has been drawn to the death of no fewer than five fathers: King Fortinbras, King Hamlet, Polonius, Priam, and Gonzago the Player King.

The demise of all these figures sounds a note that also implies its opposite; an 'avuncular' chord reverberating deep within the story. That raises its own set of ghosts. European cultures tend traditionally to establish the father as a figure of stern discipline and authority. The father's brother, the uncle, then normally occupies the structurally opposite and defining pole of laxity and good humour. This means that when Claudius seems able, even willing, to change his role from uncle to father, he's proposing a fundamental transgression, whose potential for massive desecration is mirrored by Gertrude's transformation from 'mother' to 'wife'. That Hamlet should reject Claudius's offer to 'repeat' the role of father and King should not surprise us. His withering reference to Claudius as his 'uncle-father', coupled with a no less bitter reference to Gertrude as an 'aunt-mother', announces that where they claim sameness, he registers only alarming difference.[7] But when Claudius repeats the term in Act 5, announcing that in the duel with Laertes 'Our son shall win' (5.2.289), it not only rubs salt in Hamlet's wound, it increases our sense that the Prince may have got certain things terribly wrong.

So, at the end of the play, Fortinbras's words can operate at full throttle only when uttered in this uncomfortably charged context, on a stage that contains, *inter alia*, the corpses of the 'mighty opposites', Hamlet and Claudius. Borne away together, a father who may have murdered his son, a son who may have murdered his true father whilst convinced that he was revenging him, their bodies cannot help but constitute a disturbing emblem whose political and psychological complications utterly override the inherited moral vacuities of the revenge play.

He who plays the King

In their capacity to deal with matters of such complexity, it could be said that Shakespeare's plays derive from and address themselves to a way of life still largely unwarped by the pressures at work in our own. It's one that seems to juggle with two contradictory modes, weighing an old allegiance to inherited social structures and functions against a new and competing commitment to individualism, to flushing away the past, to 'getting on', to progressive, iconoclastic 'career'-building. What Marshall McLuhan called a clash between the demands of 'roles' on the one hand and those of 'goals' on the other made the whole issue of 'playing a part' a central concern and, in the process, guaranteed the theatre the sort of critical purchase on its culture that it has not enjoyed since.[8]

Kingship and acting – the culture's two central performative modes – consequently bulk large in Shakespearean drama and each affords opportunities for a careful probing of the complexities of repetition: the ways in which some things can concurrently claim to be both 'the same' and 'different'. That is, both seem to endorse the silent presuppositions of a way of life in which the polarities of repetition (or the same) and change (or difference) operate, not as mutually exclusive opposites, but in the sort of creative, inclusive tension that challenges our own sequential logic. Thus, a defunct or deposed monarch will always be replaced by a different person, but the role at stake will always remain the same: the King is dead, long live the King. Similarly, an actor cannot avoid being both the same as, and different from, the character whose part he takes: 'This is and is not Cressid' says Troilus – of a male player – at that astonishing moment in the play when the overt pulse of the story seems to falter and role-playing bursts through as its leading subject. Drama of this sort directly challenges a reasoning which would say that someone must either be a father or an uncle, not both, and in so doing it makes possible and fosters those 'leaps' in meaning that seem so central a characteristic of the plays at large.

I'm referring to those recurrent non-discursive moments – already touched on in the discussion of bear-baiting – when the play's own continuity appears to break down and it seems suddenly to leap out at us, to burst its own boundaries, to reach beyond itself and its text, to touch us directly and often wordlessly. It's the sort of supra-textual contact with the audience in which, as has been said, 'playing' traffics. *Hamlet* is full of such moments, some of the most effective deriving from its constant reference to the act of playing.

References to the theatre in any play constitute a form of repetition, in that they reiterate a condition that the medium has already signalled. As 'repeats', their concealed investment in difference makes it impossible to naturalise or domesticate them into some regular logical progression: their effect is automatically disjunctive and the story is abruptly derailed. Thus when Polonius starts reminiscing to Hamlet about his acting career, 'I did enact Julius Caesar. I was killed i'th' Capitol. Brutus killed me' (3.2.102–3), it instantly triggers the potential implicit in those occasions when the audience perceives a particular actor or actors in one play in terms of a previous part or parts they've played in another. It must have been a not uncommon experience for regular theatre-goers in Shakespeare's day, as it is for their modern counterparts who regularly watch television or attend the cinema. Perhaps Hamlet's sly reference to the 'brute part' involved in Polonius's revelation (3.2.102–3) stresses (via 'brute' – as in Brut/Brutus) a potentially heroic dimension to this situation. Harold Jenkins notes that it certainly raises the possibility that the actor playing 'Hamlet' had already killed the actor playing 'Polonius' in a previous play (*Julius Caesar* was first performed in 1599), but its implications are much wider than that.[9] The fact that a part can be deliberately constructed, or played, to take account of audience expectations aroused by an actor's previous roles suggests casting as a major signifying stratagem of early modern plays. The repertory programme of the early modern acting companies would have encouraged this kind of canny physical troping, and it represents a keen sophistication of the expansions of meaning available *via* a particular species of repetition (its effect could also easily be exploited whenever an actor took more than one part in the same play, a practice known as 'doubling'). Suddenly, our own roles as members of an audience come to the fore. Alienated from the action of the stage, we become sharply aware both of it and of our relation to it. And when Hamlet makes his fateful promise to the Ghost,

> Remember thee?
> Ay, thou poor ghost, whiles memory holds a seat
> In this distracted globe.
>
> (1.5.95–7)

it's memorably jolting – perhaps it induces in us the sort of 'leap' in attention we call a 'double take' – when we realise that his last line refers to the theatre in which the consequences of that promise are being played out, even as he speaks.

Sceptred aisles

That was then. Whatever distracting ghosts now haunt the 'repeat' of the Globe Theatre currently adorning the South Bank of the Thames, it's a project that can hardly hope to conjure a jolting, alienating Prince of Denmark from the dark backward and abysm of time. Nor can much effective leaping be predicted. The 'new' Globe's commitment to nuts-and-bolts authenticity ensures that *déjà vu* will always hold centre-stage. In this most resolutely wooden of O's, secondariness literally comes first, and a hollow, cellaraged 'been there, done that' is likely forever to drown out more winsome cadences.

But if repetition is impossible to eradicate from our world, then it surely deserves to be openly embraced rather than occluded. The original Globe Theatre made no bones about that, and the words supposedly inscribed over its entrance seem confidently to propose copying and imitation as fundamental to the human condition. *Totus Mundus Agit Histrionem* makes players of us all. If all the world's a stage, it implies, the proper business of man-and-womankind is authentication, not authenticity. That way of life commits us to a process of reflection and repetition, the creation of a virtual world, rather than engagement with an actual one. Culture, not Nature, is our goddess. It's a point that students of the thoroughly modern (or even post-modern) should clasp firmly to the bosom. For as one of our society's most remarkable feats of recapitulation, the differences the 'new' Globe confirms say far more about us than its samenesses can possibly say about Shakespeare.

After all, in its own terms, the project rests on two conflicting principles, and our cultural logic systematically denies it a context that would enable or even encourage holding these in the creative, balanced tension characteristic of the early modern period. First, the building aims to embody, even down to the last oak shingle, the distinctive physical features of its Elizabethan predecessors. In this material sense, it welds itself firmly to a particular moment of history. Second, the exercise has been undertaken in the belief that, inherent in those theatres, at that particular moment, there existed some universal, transcendent quality capable of vaulting free from material history and of speaking to us and to future societies as intimately and as clearly as it spoke to its own.

The difficulty with the first principle is that the accuracy it aims at must be unachievable. Repetition invariably fails to produce sameness. The new Globe can never inherit the cultural role of the old one because that culture has irretrievably gone. Specifically, the new theatre can never under any circumstances recreate the single most crucial element of the Elizabethan playhouse: the audience. Like it or not, modern playgoers will almost certainly be literate, multinational, and steeled for an encounter with Great Art. An Elizabethan audience, on the other hand, was by and large non- (or pre-) literate, mainly British, and would have been surprised at our estimation of the playwright. It certainly wouldn't have recognised the fairly recent invention 'Shakespeare': that be-ruffed and bewildered-looking creature whose bland, balding likeness effortlessly endorses banknote, credit card and T-shirt. Unaware that it was in the presence of Great Art, that audience was looking for something more in the nature of what we would call entertainment. And it didn't necessarily recognise the distinctions we draw between the two.

The second principle also contains a difficulty. Literature has often been valued for its capacity to capture the supposed 'essence' of some prior period or epoch. In the particular case of drama, a play's intensely local relation to the conditions of its own production, its material involvement with actual people, on stage and in the audience, at a specific time and in a specific place, seems to help it embody its own era's deep presuppositions and make concrete its own way of life's covert prejudices and secret enthusiasms. But a true repetition of that remains, as always, impossible. As a result, for a modern audience, the one thing that Shakespeare's plays cannot help but transmit, along with their other concerns, is precisely a sense of otherness, of disparity, of the difference between the present and the past. Yet any notion of 'universality' characteristically downgrades that difference in its pursuit of 'sameness'. As was pointed out earlier, it discounts the former ('how unlike us the Elizabethans were') in order to promote the latter ('how like us the Elizabethans were'). Systematically, it requires the historically particular, the time-bound, somehow also to be transcendent and 'timeless'; the authentically Elizabethan to be simultaneously modern; the specifically and distinctively English to be able to speak unhindered and immediately to large numbers of quite different cultures, many of them surely deriving from and embodying concepts considerably older than any transmitted by an insular Bard quite ignorant, when not contemptuous, of most things foreign. One question then seems unavoidable. How can anything simultaneously be both immersed in history and drained of it?

Of course, at their most compelling, literary works do seem able to break free of the past, to leap across the centuries and speak directly to us, face to face, about matters of universal moment. They do so, it is said, by virtue of their access to a sphere that manages somehow to float freely above and beyond the material dimensions of time and place, whilst remaining to a greater or lesser degree untouched by them. Here, what is seen as their 'aesthetic' qualities hold sway and these indeed are often claimed to be a-historical, 'timeless', 'universal' or even 'transcendent' in nature. But perhaps, in the particular case of Shakespeare, some cultural sleight of hand can be detected, introducing a rather odd trump card into the aesthetic pack. If the plays are distinctively, not to say insistently, English, as well as timeless, universal and transcendent, isn't there an obvious implication? Shouldn't the world be prepared to consider, as it embarks on its unfettered, transcendent engagement with them, that this may only be feasible because it is really English too?

The truth is that the dominance of Britain by England eventually fostered a quite new idea of what being English meant. Its basis, broadened as an empire developed, lay not in one nation and its way of life, so much as in a vaguely conceived, transcendent and timeless notion of 'humanity'. Enlistment therein became one of the prizes offered by the builders of Empire to those over whom they ruled, and it also had a practical side, since the teachers on which it relied were clearly less expensive, or more expendable, than the regiments of soldiers whose functions they fulfilled. Since, as Lord Macaulay put it in 1833, 'To trade with civilised men is infinitely more profitable than to govern savages', then the most obvious stratagem must be to propagate 'that literature before the light of which impious and cruel superstitions are fast taking flight on the banks of the Ganges.'[10]

Even in the guise of industrial-strength insect-repellent, Shakespeare quickly became a major symbol of and spokesman for that kind of civilisation and the sort of cloudy, portable Englishness it embodied: one that involved less a firmly grounded way of life and scheme of values than a claim to be able to soar hygienically above the messy differences manifested by individual cultures: to be, in short, a-historical, 'timeless', 'universal' or 'transcendent'. The imperium of that Shakespeare, a Bard for all ways of life, obviously has complex links with the British Empire, and with whatever arrangements have subsequently replaced it.

But it surely comes at a heavy price if it then turns into the sort of all-purpose, multinational, evergreen Bard beloved of Hollywood, promoted by examination boards, and even memorably characterised, a few years ago, by our own Prince of Wales. Presenting an anthology of his favourite Shakespearean passages, the heir apparent commends him as, above all, one whose 'understanding of domestic life, of the minds of soldiers and politicians, of the fundamental relationships between men and women was so vast that it remains eternally relevant'.[11] The absurdity of such claims finally replaces a useful locatable Shakespeare with a flabby, vacuous monster whose promise of eternal relevance is about as trustworthy as any quack doctor's pledges concerning eternal youth. Only the Earl of Essex's famous judgement, pronounced in quite a different context, seems to do it justice: stone dead hath no fellow.

Of course, the likelihood of extinction remains remote, a prospect confirmed, if not secured, by the fact that the future guarantor, no less, of the King's English has continued to proclaim himself a Shakespeare fan. From the publication of his anthology to the foundation of an annual Prince of Wales Summer School at Stratford upon Avon, Charles's allegiance to the Bard as permanent spokesman for the finest of human values appears, despite, or perhaps because of, its expediency, to be deeply felt and genuine. Whether his appearance in the lists prefigures a larger cultural clash in which the disintegration of the United Kingdom, or of an English-speaking hegemony in the world, finally becomes an overt issue remains to be seen. Could it possibly be that the Scots, the Welsh, the Irish might at a certain point in the future come to regard an involvement with Shakespeare as somehow condoning or even embodying the 'Englishing' by which, in some eyes, they were for too long moulded?

But, in whatever tragicomedy lies ahead, there can be no doubt that the Bard, at least in his modern version, will remain a major player. We have not yet, whatever cultural materialists or new historicists might say, reached the end of the sort of blusterings that insist that his plays have a universal, non-partisan, unaligned, entirely a-political aesthetic dimension by virtue of the truth, beauty and morality that they embody. Not while Lord Marshmallow remains at large. Not while his heir (Twister Marshmallow) fidgets impatiently in the wings. Not while Hogsnorton thrives. And not while 'speaking to you in English' retains its political clout.

And so, in terms of the commitment sketched out in this book, I can in the end do no more than report my own finding that, at the present, the smart money's on the Bard's most effective representative: a shabby-genteel figure, whose cut-glass accent, faded blazer and funny stories about quaint goings on in a wholly imaginary location seem paradoxically to offer the unmistakable signs of failure. Of course, he never really fails, and that's the point. In fact, at the moment, he looks suspiciously like the person most likely to succeed.

Notes

1 Introduction

1 See Kastan (1999: 15–17).
2 See Kastan (1999: 17). For a more detailed account and critique of presentism see Wells (2000).
3 See Kastan (1999: 38).
4 The fact that there currently exists no parliament for England is one major anomaly that results.

2 The Heimlich Manoeuvre

1 Arnold (1962: 273).
2 Arnold (1962: 274).
3 Arnold (1962: 479).
4 Eliot (1951: 27).
5 Eliot (1951: 27).
6 I am here and in what follows drawing extensively on Andrew Thacker's provocative argument: see Thacker (1993: 224–46).
7 See Thacker (1993: 239–40).
8 Usually translated as 'The Uncanny'. See Freud (1963).
9 I am aware that the modern German word *heimlich* does not necessarily carry the sense that the Austrian Freud seems to ascribe to it. His detailed philological analysis covers several pages and is none the less remarkably thorough. Its aim, of course, is less to specify individual meanings than to focus on the spurious 'opposition' of *heimlich* and *unheimlich*.
10 Freud (1963: 220).
11 Freud (1963: 241–5).
12 Freud (1963: 220).
13 Freud (1963: 224–5).
14 Freud (1963: 226). This classic deconstructive analysis perhaps lingered to haunt the German language in the twenty years following Freud's paper. At its furthest reach, *heimlich* has links not only with

Heimat, the 'homeland', but even perhaps – via *geheim* – with the secret forces of terror raised to exclude the *Heimat*'s enemies. This generates a kind of oxymoron whose grim climax occurred when Freud joked of the *Geheime Staatspolizei,* after they had ransacked his *heimlich* Vienna home, that he could 'heartily recommend the Gestapo to anybody'. See Jones (1964: 642).

15 Said (1984: 12).

16 Arnold (1962: 273). Christopher Ricks has commented on Eliot's no less intense interest in such matters. Certainly, Eliot's inventions for the correspondence columns of *The Egoist* include names that would have confirmed Arnold's despair: 'Charles James Grimble (The Vicarage, Leays)' and 'Helen B. Trundlett (Batton, Kent)', to say nothing of 'Muriel A. Schwarz (60, Alexandra Gardens, Hampstead NW)'. Note also Eliot's constant invention of names in the spirit of *nomen est omen*: Professor Channing-Cheetah, Nancy Ellicott and, supremely, J. Alfred Prufrock. Of course Eliot also had his *trouvailles* to match Arnold's Wragg and Roebuck, such as Sir Alfred Mond. See Ricks (1988: 1–24, 242–3).

17 Foucault (1981: 52–64). See also Foucault (1970: 78–81).

18 Freud (1963: 234).

19 *Das Unheimliche* itself presents a valuable complication of the matter for the actual writing of it is so saturated with the issues of repetition that they begin to call into question the very principles on which parts of the argument seem to rest. The War itself had of course decisively undermined linear notions of sequence and consequence. It is, Freud says, as a result of the 'times in which we live' that he presents his paper 'without any claim to priority' (Freud 1963: 220). In a letter to Ferenczi in May 1919 he indicates directly that he has dug an old paper out of a drawer and is rewriting it (p.218), whereupon the editors of the Standard edition admit that 'Nothing is known as to when it was originally written or how much it was changed'. They even contribute the straight-faced comment that 'The passages dealing with the "compulsion to repeat" must in any case have formed part of the revision' (p.218). In short, Freud's revisionary return to the paper means that a crumbling of the primary–secondary relationship characterises the very composition of the argument before surfacing as one of its most disturbing features.

20 I take the phrase from Luke Gibbons's invaluable essay: Gibbons (1991).

21 See Hill (1986: 169–70).

22 Arnold (1962: 273–4).

23 See Gibbons (1991). There was a notable rise in cases of recorded infanticide in Britain in the 1860s, together with a tendency to regard the crime as an 'Irish' solution to the problem of poverty – a point of view informed perhaps by recollections of Swift's *A Modest Proposal*. See Sauer (1978). I am indebted to Dr Jo McDonagh of the University of Exeter for this and a great deal more information on the topic.

24 See Said (1984: 8, 17). On Eliot's marriage see Seymour-Jones (2001).
25 See Rook (1979: especially 14–20).
26 See Wilde (1970: *passim*).
27 Wilde (1970: 403).
28 Adorno (1951: 38–9).

3 Bryn Glas

1 A recent historian has incisively presented the two versions of Wales in terms of two different modes of entry into, or readings of, the Principality, which chart its culture from two opposed points of view: on the one hand that of an English official, reliant on the stepping-stones of towns and castles, but otherwise alienated and at risk in a remote and unintelligibly foreign country, and on the other that of a native Welsh-speaking poet whose 'bardic' role involves precisely the weaving, using legend, myth and genealogy, of a coherent vision of national identity. See Davies (1995: 5–34).
2 Henken (1996) gives an authoritative account of the role in folk-lore of the Glyn Dŵr figure, both as redeemer and trickster, throughout Welsh history.
3 Holinshed (1587: 3: 520).
4 Holinshed (1587: 3: 528).
5 See Williams (1985: 117).
6 Williams (1985: 119).
7 The idea of Britain as a separate but coherent 'world the world without' is discussed in Edwards (1979: 87–8) and Wind (1967: 224–30).
8 Williams (1985: 121–3).
9 Williams (1985: 121).
10 Williams (1985: 123–4).
11 Williams (1985: 124–6).
12 See Humphreys (1960: xxvi).
13 In view of Hotspur's notoriously 'thick' speech, this may be less of an achievement than Glendower supposes.
14 See Davies (1995: 107–8) for an authoritative account of the battle. The 'beastly' Circean transformation wrought by the Welsh on the English was evidently a fundamental one, its implications powerful enough to initiate a theme of metamorphosis that Shakespeare's whole tetralogy extrapolates. In these plays, ordinary humans such as Bolingbroke can be transformed into kings and it seems almost reasonable for the King to hope that some 'night-tripping fairy' might turn out to have transformed his son (1.1.85–8). Human beings can be transformed into animals (3.1.142–55), the course of rivers can be transformed by dams, the whole island of Britain can be transformed by the plans of the rebels, and, as the climax of the process, the madcap Hal is ultimately transformed into Henry V.

15 Glendower's Welshness of course needs no demonstration. His standing as native 'Prince of Wales' is variously emphasised, as, for instance, when immediately after his exit at the end of the plotting scene (3.1), the King enters, with Hal, saying 'Lords, give us leave; The Prince of Wales and I/Must have some private conference...' (3.2.1–2). Clearly the title 'Prince of Wales' is a disputable one and Glendower's claims to it raise the issue. Not insignificantly, Falstaff's most eloquent plea for his own preservation comes when he too is playing the part of 'Prince of Wales' (2.4.469–74). Glendower's entry, moments after Falstaff has been discovered behind the arras asleep, and at his most grotesquely dilapidated, even suggests the possibility of doubling these two roles to underline, silently but effectively, their connection.

16 Sinfield (1992: 131). See also Traub (1992).

17 See Humphreys (1960: xii–xiii; xvi–xviii; xxxix and lxviff.). Oldcastle's situation is described in Holinshed (1587: 2: 544, 560). Conflicting versions of his story paint him either as scoundrel or 'valiant martyr' depending on the religious viewpoint at stake (an indeterminacy which the play perhaps encourages). However, Oldcastle's name was changed because Sir Henry Brooke, Lord Cobham, or his father Sir William Brooke – both descendants of the historical Oldcastle – objected, early in 1597, to the depiction of their ancestor as a reprobate. The character was then given the name of Sir John Fastolf (1378–1459), one of Henry V's leaders who fought well at Agincourt. However, at the battle of Patay, he deserted Talbot, who was captured as a result. The *Sir John Oldcastle* play admits that its hero had been travestied.

18 See Davies (1995: 300–1).

19 See Edwards (1979: 74–86). Edwards's account of the play's 'conviction ... of the dominance of England' (p.74) perhaps underestimates the doubts and insecurities the project of 'Great Britain' was capable of engendering amongst all parties involved.

20 Cf. 'Sense contaminates this non-sense that is supposed to be kept aside; the name is not supposed to signify anything, yet it does begin to signify', Derrida (1977: 146). See Culler (1983: 192–3).

21 See Williams (1985: 119).

22 Davies (1995: 129). Glyn Dŵr's full Welsh name was Owain ap Gruffudd, or Owain Glyn Dŵr, Owain of Glyndyfrdwy. His cognomen derives from his connection with the manor of Glyndyfrdwy (Glendowerdy) in the Dee valley in Wales. See Williams (1985: 106) and Davies (1995: 1).

23 Williams (1985: 114).

24 T.W. Craik offers the strange comment that 'Fluellen' is 'an anglicized spelling of Llewelyn (sic) ... that prevents incorrect pronunciation', Craik (1995: 205). See also Craik (1995: 111).

25 I take the view that the killing is not mitigated by being a response to the French attack on the boys: the command is issued before that event. This matter and the larger issue of Henry's 'coldbloodedness' is discussed in Taylor (1984: 32–3).

26 See Edwards (1979: 74ff.). See also Murphy (1996: 38–59) and Baldo (1996: 132–59).
27 See Edwards (1979: 205–11).

4 Aberdaugleddyf

1 See Rees (1954: 2).
2 Popular etymology suggests that the name is taken from a stream that turned a mill over which there was a ford. See Lewis (1849: 2: 215–17).
3 Of course, this is impossibly unfair both to Miss Jones and her creator Mara Purl, whose account of the origin of 'Milford Haven' (communicated privately) indicates none the less a link with *Cymbeline*, a play in which Ms Purl has performed as an actress. I am also heavily indebted to Mr Louis J. Slovinsky for information concerning the soap opera and the published versions of its stories.
4 Shaw (1896), Johnson (1969: 136).
5 Rees (1954: 3).
6 See Lewis (1849: 216).
7 Not suprisingly, Milford Haven's role is confirmed in the many anecdotes and myths that commemorate Richmond's landing there. See Lewis (1849: 215). See also Williams (1925: 64–5).
8 See Carlisle (1811: 3N, 3N2). Cf. J.F. Rees: 'All references to Milford Haven are variations on the theme that there has been persistent failure to make use of the facilities it offers' (Rees, 1954: 1).
9 See Edwards (1979: 87–8).
10 Edwards (1979: 135).
11 See Edwards (1979: 71).
12 See Jones (1961).
13 See Edwards (1979: 83).
14 See Jones (1961: 90, 92). Jones also points out that Brute's wife, the first queen of Britain, was named Innogen (p.99).
15 See Jones (1961: 92–9).
16 See Warren (1998: v: 4–5).
17 Knight (1948: 183).
18 Knight (1948: 139ff., 164).
19 *Cit.* Warren (1998: 64).
20 See Edwards (1979: 92–4).
21 On Snow White, see Warren (1998: 16).
22 *OED* indicates that early modern English contained both these possibilities.
23 27 Henry VIII, c.26, 1536; Bowen, *Statutes*, pp.75–6. *Cit.* Herbert and Jones (1988: 149–50).
24 *Cit.* Edwards (1979: 1).
25 At present, as has been pointed out, the question of an 'English' parliament remains unresolved.
26 Knight (1948: 139–45 and 164).
27 See Woolf and Wilson (1982: 66–7).

28 Knight's further judgement that, in the closing scenes of the play, the Roman eagle is seen 'leaving a soft, effete, decaying land for one more virile' (Knight 1948: 166) will also be tempered by a presentist perception that Knight's essay, published after the Second World War, marks exactly the point in time at which the mantle of empire in the Western world seemed decisively to fall from British shoulders on to those of the United States.

29 See Johnson and Malone (1931: VI, 487–8).

5 The Old Bill

1 I am greatly indebted to Professor Balz Engler who has kindly made his extensive knowledge of these matters available to me. Further details can be found in Lange (1980) especially pp.321–2; Stahl (1947) and Hortmann (1998). For an incisive and judicious analysis of this 'massive theatre programme' in its larger political context as part of the 'American response to the Soviet cultural offensive' see Saunders (1999: 20–1). Ms Saunders's witty and provocative account of the cultural politics of the post-war world is illuminating on a large scale. I am extremely grateful to her for affording me access to copies of relevant documents.

2 Curiously, on 3 May 2000, the police eventually agreed to a declaration in the High Court that a number of their actions during the state visit of President Jiang Zemin had in fact been 'unlawful'.

3 The term 'The Old Bill' or 'The Bill' is nineteenth-century British thieves' slang for the police. It has now passed, through a television-driven process of gentrification, into polite parlance.

4 See Chambers (1933: 179–80). It is scarcely necessary to point out the *Hamlet* echoes of Agatha Christie's ingenious detective play *The Mousetrap*.

5 Greg (1960: 12–17). Greg's friend Frank Elliott was an 'assistant commissioner' at the Yard. See Wilson, F.P. (1959: 307–34, 320). See also Wilson, John Dover (1959: 153–7).

6 See Wilson, F.P. (1959: 331).

7 We can discount immediately the less generous conclusion of some editors that such a case merely represents the vestigial, interpolated remains of an actor's actual difficulty, encountered in performance, and should thus rank as a theatrical 'accretion' to the text, as Harold Jenkins terms it. See Jenkins (1982: 62). His rather odd judgement is that the Folio text is using 'extra words' here, which 'though they have usually been regarded as an omission in Q2, have the air of an actor's elaboration' (p.232). In addition to driving a wholly illegitimate wedge between text and performance, the notion of 'accretion' awards 'the text' a pride of place that commits the play to the study rather than the theatre. Worse, it risks missing a key moment where, once again, the play rather than one of its characters speaks.

8 See Jenkins (1982: 482–3).

9 Jenkins (1982) gives a full account of these in his 'long note', pp.501–5.
10 Jenkins (1982: 508). See also pp.145, 156.
11 This point has most recently been made by Grady (1996: 4–25).
12 See Eliot (1951: 141–6), and Eliot (1964: 44). Of course, on one level, this is a mere debating point. Each set of judgements was made for quite different reasons and in completely different contexts. The symmetry is nevertheless startling.
13 For a full account of Reiss's life see Haider-Pregler (1998). I am heavily indebted to Professor Haider-Pregler's work and she was also kind enough to make a good deal of information available to me privately. A play about Reiss, by Felix Mitterer, *In der Löwengrube*, opened on 14 January 1999 in the Badisches Landestheater in Karlsruhe.
14 Schnitzler (1998: 14, 92). On the subject of Schnitzler's situation as a Jew and the Jewish dimension of Vienna, see Raphael (1999: v–xvii).
15 See, for example, Hilsky (1994) and Gibinska (1994).
16 The letter is dated 12 May 1945 and is included in the file OMGUS/RG260/Box 242/NARA, National Archives, Washington, DC.

6 Harry Hunks, Superstar

1 *Cit.* Chambers (1923: 2: 455).
2 In making and pursuing this point, and more generally, I am greatly indebted to the work of S.P. Cerasano (Cerasano 1991) and of Meredith Anne Skura (Skura 1993). I would nevertheless question Cerasano's conclusion that 'baiting was perceived as a form of diversion quite distinct from playing' (p.196).
3 Stubbes (1583: 115–16).
4 Thomas (1983: 157–8).
5 Thomas (1983: 191).
6 *Cit.* Lee (1916: 432).
7 Paul Hentzner's account of his travels in Germany, France, England and Italy (in Latin 1598, 1612), quoted in Wilson (1944: 207–8).
8 See Chambers (1923: 2: 456).
9 See Chambers (1923: 2: 355, 450). Ironically, Philip Henslowe's papers record an advertisement or 'bill' of the entertainment available on one afternoon at the Bear Garden which concludes as follows: '...and for your better content shall have pleasant sport with the horse and ape and whipping of the blind beare. Viuat Rex. (Chambers 1923: 2: 458).
10 See Lee (1916: 429).
11 See Chambers (1923: 2: 452–4).
12 See Cerasano (1991: 203–4).
13 Chambers (1923: 2: 466).

14 *Cit.* Chambers (1923: 2: 457, n.6).
15 Thomas (1983: 114).
16 The quotation is from Henry Peacham, *Coryats Crudities* (1611), *cit.* Chambers (1923: 2: 457, n.7).
17 Chambers (1923: 4: 270, 294).
18 See Chambers (1923: 4: 311, 313–15, 335ff.).
19 Stubbes (1583: 87, 88, 94, 98, 107, 115, 120).
20 Thomas Dekker, 'Warres' in *Worke for Armourers, or, the Peace is Broken* (1609), *cit.* Skura (1993: 204, 306, n.10). In 1612, on the death of the Prince of Wales, the Privy Council proposed to the Lord Mayor of London the suppression of all 'Playes, shewes, Bearebaytinges, or any other such sighte' on the grounds that 'these tymes doe not suite with such playes and idle shewes...' Chambers (1923: 4: 341).
21 Chambers (1923: 2: 471). See also Chambers (1923: 4: 307).
22 Metaphors drawn from the practice are everywhere and inform all manner of encounters. Joseph Swetnam's tract *The Arraignment of Lewd, Idle, Froward and Unconstant Women* virtually enacts a visit to the arena in his initial 'greeting' to the reader: 'If thou meanest to see the Bear-bayting of Women, then trudge to this Beare-garden apace, and get in betymes, and view every roome, where thou mayest best sit for thine owne pleasure, profit, and hearts-ease...' In fact, the last section of the pamphlet is entitled 'The Beare-bayting, or the vanities of Widdowes: chuse you whether'. Swetnam (1645: A4, 57–63).
23 See Skura (1993: 227).
24 Skura (1993: 203).
25 On the use of charivari or 'rough music' as a form of public harassment, see Davies (1971) and Thompson (1972).
26 See Skura (1993: 306, n.2). As Steven Mullaney says of the society's treatment of lepers, 'the institution of the lazar house reminds us, as it once reminded leprosy's contemporaries, that the lazar's life as a spectacle was initiated rather than concluded by his passage out of the city'. Mullaney (1988: 36).
27 Skura (1993: 7).
28 'Like any art form – for that, finally, is what we are dealing with – the cockfight renders ordinary, everyday experience comprehensible by presenting it in terms of acts and objects which have had their practical consequences removed and been reduced (or, if you prefer, raised) to the level of sheer appearances, where their meaning can be more powerfully articulated and more exactly perceived ... Enacted and re-enacted ... the cockfight enables the Balinese, as, read and reread, *Macbeth* enables us, to see a dimension of his own subjectivity.' Geertz (1993: 450). Of course, Shakespeare did not shrink from referring to his own theatre as a 'cockpit' (*Henry V*, Prologue 11–12).
29 *Cit.* Chambers (1923: 2: 457, n.4).
30 On this notion of 'law' see Eagleton (1986: 35–63).
31 See Leggatt (1994: 46–51). Leggatt's otherwise perceptive and

informative argument that the one practice informs or contaminates the other, so that bear-baiting provides the drama with metaphorical content, strikes me as possibly misleading in some of its fundamental presuppositions. First, it personalises and so risks reducing the issue to a matter of individual preference, speculating that Shakespeare found bear-baiting 'useful in his work' and that he 'was fascinated by it, and his imagination was affected by it'. Second, it sees bear-baiting as illuminating the plays. But rather than awarding primacy to one, it would surely be more appropriate to probe the interdependent relationship pertaining between all the elements of the ensemble. The view that bear-baiting illuminates the plays doesn't quite engage with this because of its implicit privileging of the theatre. It might no less persuasively be argued that the plays illuminate bear-baiting.

32 Ralph Berry makes this point most effectively (Berry, 1981: 118).

33 Polixenes's opening lines appear to set the standard for a transparent linguistic 'normality' on the stage:

> Nine changes of the watery star hath been
> The shepherd's note since we have left our throne ... [etc.]
>
> (1.2.1ff.)

But then, moments later, a cacophony of self-reflexive utterances starts to take up the subject of language itself. It lasts for several minutes and ranges from Leontes's obsessive urging of his wife to speak to Polixenes in order to persuade him to stay, 'Tongue-tied, our Queen? Speak you' (1.2.28) through an interchange between Hermione and Polixenes which offers a virtual disquisition on the veridical capacities of the term 'verily' (1.2.45–55) into a related discussion between Hermione and Leontes on speaking 'to the purpose' and the power of language to mobilise intention and to make things happen (1.2.87–107).

34 See Eagleton (1986: 55).

35 Coghill's discussion as to whether the bear is real, or an actor wearing a bear-skin, is not altogether relevant here (Coghill 1958). My conclusion would be that the initial production used a genuine bear.

36 Compare Jeanne Addison Roberts's conclusion that, in *The Winter's Tale*, the bear liberates the play world from the 'tyranny of male culture' by its preservation of a female child (Roberts 1991: 83).

37 See Pafford (1966: lxxxi, n.7).

38 We first meet Florizel and Perdita donning 'unusual weeds' that alter their supposed class status:.

> Your high self
> The gracious mark o' th' land, you have obscured
> With a swain's wearing; and me, poor lowly maid,
> Most goddesslike pranked up
>
> (4.4.7–10)

Florizel's justification of the disguise is permitted its full unpleas-
antness:

> The gods themselves,
> Humbling their deities to love, have taken
> The shapes of beasts upon them. Jupiter
> Became a bull, and bellowed; the green Neptune
> A ram, and bleated; and the fire-robed god,
> Golden Apollo, a poor humble swain,
> As I seem now.'
>
> (4.4.25–31)

39 Autolycus's mockery of the class-divisions at stake is never less than
   caustic, employing a biting irony echoed by the clown whose
   response to his new attire reinforces Autolycus's own, e.g., 'You
   are well met sir. You denied to fight with me this other day,
   because I was no gentleman born. See you these clothes? Say you
   see them not and think me still no gentleman born; you were best
   say these robes are not gentlemen born...' (5.2.127–31).
40 See Eagleton (1986: 55ff.).
41 The manuscript here displays the symbol for Mercury = Wednes-
   day.
42 'away'?
43 coll pixci = colt-pixie: a mischievous sprite?
44 See the entry by Sidney Lee in the *Dictionary of National Biography*,
   vol. XIX, London 1889. Lee admits, rather grudgingly, that
   Forman did obtain a medical qualification from Jesus College,
   Cambridge, in 1603. See also Traister (2001) for a much more balanced and judicious assessment, including an account of Forman's
   unpublished manuscripts.
45 See Rowse (1974).
46 Rowse (1974: 24).
47 See 5.2.114ff.
48 See Wimsatt (1969: 109). Also Pafford (1966: lxxxi). Pafford calls
   Johnson's judgement 'high praise indeed'.
49 See Pafford (1966: lxxix, n.5).
50 Cf. Grady (1996: 33–57).

7 Hank Cinq

1 Grahame (1944: 33).
2 Grahame (1944: 33).
3 John Stephens, *Satyrical Essayes Characters and Others* (London
  1615). *Cit.* Weimann (2000: 135). What follows owes a considerable
  debt to Weimann's detailed and extremely fruitful account of the
  material developments underlying the difference between 'playing'
  and 'acting' (see especially pp.131–6). The important relationship
  of this distinction to the stage areas *locus* and *platea*, previously identified and explored by Weimann in his ground-breaking *Shakespeare*

and the Popular Tradition in the Theatre (Weimann 1978), is pursued on pp.180–208.

4 Weimann's incisive discussion of this distinction is crucial. See Weimann (2000: 131–2).

5 See Alter (1990: 32) and Weimann (2000: 106).

6 See Weimann (2000: 5).

7 See Brecht (1964: 136–43 and 193–200).

8 See Weimann (2000: 70–5) Cf. Brecht (1964: 22–42).

9 Bethell (1944: 38).

10 Something that the title of a lost play performed thirteen times by the Admiral's company between 28 November 1595 and 15 July 1596 confirms: it was *Harry the V*.

11 Bloom (1999: 3).

12 Cf. Carr (1964: 43).

13 *Cit.* Taylor (1990: 166).

14 See Taylor (1990: 165).

15 For information about aspects of Furnivall's private life see Thompson (1998).

16 See Benzie (1983: 179–220).

17 *Cit.* Benzie (1983: 180).

18 See Benzie (1983: 206).

19 See Benzie (1983: 192).

20 *Cit.* Benzie (1983: 182).

21 *Cit.* Benzie (1983: 183).

22 *Cit.* Benzie (1983: 198).

23 *Cit.* Benzie (1983: 199ff.).

24 See Munro (1911: 75–7).

25 *Cit.* Benzie (1983: 208).

26 See Hawkes (1986: 117–18).

27 See Hartman (1980: 4 and *passim*).

8 Conclusion: Speaking to You in English

1 Knight (1940: 31–2, 34).

2 Knight (1940: 32, 35).

3 Schwarz (1996). See also my review of this volume, Hawkes (1997).

4 Borges (1965: 49).

5 Kierkegaard (1983: 149).

6 Deleuze (1968: xix).

7 For a fuller discussion of this issue in a different context, see Hawkes (1986: 99–101).

8 See McLuhan (1962: 14–18).

9 See Jenkins (1982: 294, n.).

10 See Baldick (1983: 70–1).

11 Wales (1995: 3).

References

Adorno, Theodor (1951) *Minima Moralia: Reflections from Damaged Life*, trans. E.F.N. Jephcott, London: New Left Books.

Alter, Jean (1990) *A Sociosemiotic Theory of Theater*, Philadelphia: University of Pennsylvania Press.

Arnold, Matthew (1962) *Lectures and Essays in Criticism*, ed. R.H. Super, *The Complete Prose Works of Matthew Arnold*, vol. 3, Ann Arbor: University of Michigan Press.

Baldick, Chris (1983) *The Social Mission of English Criticism 1848–1932*, Oxford: The Clarendon Press.

Baldo, Jonathan (1996) 'Wars of Memory in *Henry V*, *Shakespeare Quarterly* 47, 2: 132–59.

Benzie, William (1983) *Dr. F. J. Furnivall, Victorian Scholar Adventurer*, Norman, Oklahoma: Pilgrim Books.

Berry, Ralph (1981) 'Twelfth Night: The Experience of the Audience', *Shakespeare Survey* 34: 111–19.

Bethell, S.L. (1944) *Shakespeare and the Popular Dramatic Tradition*, London: Staples.

Bloom, Harold (1999) *Shakespeare, The Invention of the Human*, London: Fourth Estate.

Borges, Jorge Luis (1965) *Fictions*, ed. Anthony Kerrigan, London: John Calder.

Brecht, Bertolt (1964) *Brecht on Theatre*, trans. John Willett, London: Methuen.

Carlisle, Nicholas (1811) *Topographical Dictionary of the Dominion of Wales*, London.

Carr, E.H. (1964) *What is History?*, Harmondsworth: Penguin.

Cerasano S.P. (1991) 'The Master of the Bears in Art and Enterprise', *Medieval and Renaissance Drama in England*, vol. 5: 195–209.

Chambers, E.K. (1923) *The Elizabethan Stage*, 4 vols. Oxford: Clarendon Press.

Chambers, E.K. (1933) *A Short Life of Shakespeare* (abridged by Charles Williams), Oxford: The Clarendon Press.

Coghill, Neville (1958) 'Six Points of Stage-Craft in The Winter's Tale', *Shakespeare Survey* 11: pp. 31–41.

Craik, T.W. (1995) ed., *Henry V*, London: Routledge (the Arden edition).

Culler, Jonathan (1983) *On Deconstruction*, London: Routledge.

Davies, R.R. (1995) *The Revolt of Owain Glyn Dŵr*, Oxford: Oxford University Press.

Davies, Natalie Zemon (1971) 'The Reasons of Misrule: Youth Groups and Charivaris in 16th Century France', *Past and Present* 50: 49–75.

Deleuze, Gilles (1968) *Difference and Repetition* trans. Paul Patton, London: Athlone Press.

Derrida, Jacques (1977) 'Signeponge' Part 1, in *Francis Ponge: Colloque de Cerisy*, Paris: Union Generale d'Editions.

Eagleton, Terry (1986) *William Shakespeare*, Oxford: Blackwell.

Edwards, Philip (1979) *Threshold of a Nation*, Cambridge: Cambridge University Press.

Eliot, T.S. (1964) *The Use of Poetry and the Use of Criticism*, London: Faber & Faber (first pub. 1933).

Eliot, T.S. (1951) *Selected Essays*, 3rd edn, London: Faber & Faber.

Foucault, Michel (1970) *The Order of Things: An Archaeology of the Human Sciences*, London, Tavistock Publications.

Foucault, Michel (1981) 'The Order of Discourse' in Robert Young, ed., *Untying the Text*, London: Routledge, pp. 52–64.

Freud, Sigmund (1963) *Complete Psychological Works*, vol. xvii, Standard Edition, ed. James Strachey, London: Hogarth, pp. 217–56.

Geertz, Clifford (1993) *The Interpretation of Cultures*, London: Fontana.

Gibbons, Luke (1991) 'Race Against Time: Racial Discourse and Irish History', *Oxford Literary Review*, 13: 98.

Gibinska, Marta (1994) 'Polish Hamlets: Shakespeare's *Hamlet* in Polish theatres after 1945' in Hattaway *et al.*, pp. 159–73.

Grady, Hugh (1996) *Shakespeare's Universal Wolf: Studies in Early Modern Reification*, Oxford: Clarendon Press.

Grahame, Kenneth (1944) *The Wind in the Willows*, London: Methuen, 1908 (75th edn).

Greg, W.W. (1960) *Biographical Notes 1877–1947*, Oxford: New Bodleian Library.

Haider-Pregler, Hilde (1998) *Überlebens-Theater. Der Schauspieler Reuss.* Vienna: Holzhausen Verlag.

Hartman, Geoffrey (1980) *Criticism in the Wilderness*, New Haven: Yale University Press.

Hattaway, Michael, Sokolova, Boika and Roper, Derek (1994) (eds) *Shakespeare in the New Europe*, Sheffield: Sheffield Academic Press.

Hawkes, Terence (1986) *That Shakespeherean Rag: essays on a critical process*, London and New York: Methuen.

Hawkes, Terence (1997) 'Making = Taking', *London Review of Books*, 19:15, 31 July 1997, pp. 16–17.

Henken, Elissa R. (1996) *National Redeemer, Owain Glyn Dŵr in Welsh Tradition*, Cardiff: University of Wales Press.

Herbert, Trevor and Jones, Gareth Elwyn (1988) (eds) *Tudor Wales*, Cardiff: University of Wales Press.

Hill, Christopher (1986) *People and Ideas in 17th Century England*, Brighton: Harvester.

Hilsky, Martin (1994) 'Shakespeare in Czech: an essay in cultural semantics' in Hattaway *et al.*, pp. 150–8.

Holinshed, Raphael (1587) *The Chronicles of England, Scotland and Ireland*, London: 1587, 3 vols, in 2.

Hortmann, Wilhelm (1998) *Shakespeare on the German Stage, Vol. 2: the Twentieth Century*, Cambridge: Cambridge University Press.

Humphreys, A.R. (1960) (ed.) *Henry IV Part 1*, London: Methuen (the Arden edition).

Jenkins, Harold (1982) (ed.) *Hamlet*, London and New York: Methuen (the Arden edition).

Johnson, Allen and Malone, Dumas (1931) (eds) *Dictionary of American Biography*, London: Oxford University Press.

Johnson, Samuel (1969: 136) *The Plays of William Shakespeare* (London: 1765), *cit.* W.K. Wimsatt (ed.) *Dr. Johnson on Shakespeare*, Harmondsworth: Penguin.

Jones, Emrys (1961) 'Stuart Cymbeline', *Essays in Criticism*, 11: 84–99.

Jones, Ernest (1964) *The Life and Work of Sigmund Freud*, Harmondsworth: Penguin.

Kastan, David (1999) *Shakespeare After Theory*, New York and London: Routledge.

Kierkegaard, Soren (1983) *Repetition*, trans. Howard V. Hong and Edna H. Hong, Princeton, NJ: Princeton University Press.

Knight, G. Wilson (1940) *This Sceptred Isle: Shakespeare's Message for England at War*, Oxford: Basil Blackwell.

Knight, G. Wilson (1948) *The Crown of Life*, London: Methuen, 1965, p. 135.

Lange, Wigand (1980) *Theater in Deutschland nach 1945: Zur Theaterpolitik der Amerikanischen Besatzungsbehörden*, Frankfurt: Peter Lang.

Lee, Sidney (1916) 'Bearbaiting, Bullbaiting and Cockfighting' in *Shakespeare's England, an Account of the Life and Manners of His Age*, Oxford: Clarendon Press, vol. ii, pp. 428–36.

Leggatt, Alexander (1994) 'Shakespeare and Bearbaiting' in Tetsuo Kishi, Roger Pringle and Stanley Wells (eds) *Shakespeare and Cultural Traditions, The Selected Proceedings of the International Shakespeare Association World Congress, Tokyo, 1991*, Newark, London, Toronto: University of Delaware Press, pp. 43–53.

Lewis, Samuel (1849) *A Topographical Dictionary of Wales*, London, vol. 2.

McLuhan, Marshall (1962) *The Gutenberg Galaxy: The Making of Typographic Man*, London: Routledge.

Mullaney, Steven (1988) *The Place of the Stage*, Chicago: University of Chicago Press.

Munro, John (1911) (ed.) *Frederick James Furnivall: A Volume of Personal Record*, Oxford: Oxford University Press.

Murphy, Andrew (1996) 'Shakespeare's Irish History', *Literature and History*, 3: 5: 1.

Pafford, J.H.P. (1966) (ed.) *The Winter's Tale*, London: Methuen (the Arden edition).

Raphael, Fredric (1999) Introduction to Arthur Schnitzler *Dream Story* (1926), London: Penguin.

Rees, J.F. (1954) *The Story of Milford*, Cardiff: University of Wales Press.

Ricks, Christopher (1988) *T.S. Eliot and Prejudice*, London: Faber & Faber.

Roberts, Jeanne Addison (1991) *The Shakespearean Wild: Geography, Genus, and Gender*, Lincoln: University of Nebraska Press.

Rook, Clarence (1979) *The Hooligan Nights* (1899), Oxford: Oxford University Press.

Rowse, A.L. (1974) *The Case Books of Simon Forman: Sex and Society in Shakespeare's Age*, London: Weidenfeld and Nicolson.

Said, Edward (1984) *The World, the Text, and the Critic*, London: Faber & Faber.

Sauer, R. (1978) 'Deadly Motherhood: Infanticide and Abortion in 19th century Britain', *Population Studies*, 32: 81–93.

Saunders, Frances Stonor (1999) *Who Paid the Piper: The CIA and the Cultural Cold War*, London: Granta Books.

Schnitzler, Arthur (1998) *Fräulein Else*, trans. F.H. Lyon (1925), London: Pushkin Press.

Schwarz, Hillel (1996) *The Culture of the Copy: Striking Likenesses, Unreasonable Facsimiles*, New York: Zone Books.

Seymour-Jones, Carole (2001) *Painted Shadow: A Life of Vivienne Eliot*, London: Constable.

Shaw, George Bernard (1896) 'Blaming the Bard', *The Saturday Review*, September 16.

Sinfield, Alan (1992) *Faultlines; Cultural Materialism and the Politics of Dissident Reading*, Oxford: Clarendon Press.

Skura, Meredith Ann (1993) *Shakespeare the Actor and the Purposes of Playing*, Chicago and London: University of Chicago Press.

Stahl, Ernst Leopold (1947) *Shakespeare und das Deutsche Theater*, Stuttgart: Kohlhammer.

Stubbes, Philip (1583) *The Anatomie of Abuses*, London.

Swetnam, Joseph (1645 edition) *The Arraignment of Lewd, Idle, Froward and Unconstant Women*, London. B. Lib. C.136. f.18.

Taylor, Gary (1984) (ed.) *Henry V*, Oxford: Oxford University Press (The Oxford Shakespeare).

Taylor, Gary (1990) *Reinventing Shakespeare: A Cultural History from the Restoration to the Present*, London: The Hogarth Press.

Thacker, Andrew (1993) 'Imagist Travels In Modernist Space', *Textual Practice*, 7: 2: 224–46.

Thomas, Keith (1983) *Man and the Natural World: Changing Attitudes in England 1500–1800*, London: Alan Lane.

Thompson, Ann (1998) 'Teena Rochfort Smith, Frederick Furnivall, and the New Shakespere Society's Four-Text Edition of Hamlet', *Shakespeare Quarterly* 49: 2: 125–39.

Thompson, E.P. (1972) 'Rough Music: Le charivari Anglais', *Annales: Economies, Sociétés, Civilisation*, 27: 285–312.

Traister, Barbara Howard (2001) *The Notorious Astrological Physician of*

London: Works and Days of Simon Forman, Chicago and London: University of Chicago Press.

Traub, Valerie (1992) *Desire and Anxiety: Circulations of Sexuality in Shakespearean Drama*, London: Routledge.

Wales, HRH Charles, Prince of (1995) *The Prince's Choice, a Personal Selection from Shakespeare with an Introduction by HRH the Prince Of Wales*, London, Hodder and Stoughton.

Warren, Roger (1998) (ed.) *Cymbeline*, Oxford: Oxford University Press (The Oxford Shakespeare).

Weimann, Robert (2000) *Author's Pen and Actor's Voice*, Cambridge: Cambridge University Press.

Weimann, Robert (1978) *Shakespeare and the Popular Tradition in the Theatre*, Baltimore: Johns Hopkins University Press.

Wells, R. Headlam (2000) 'Historicism and 'presentism' in early modern studies', *The Cambridge Quarterly*, 29: 1: 37–60.

Wilde, Oscar (1970) Richard Ellmann (ed.) *The Artist as Critic: Critical Writings of Oscar Wilde*, London, W.H. Allen: 355–403.

Williams, E. Rowland (1925) *Some Studies of Elizabethan Wales*, Newtown, Montgomeryshire: The Welsh Outlook Press.

Williams, Gwyn A. (1985) *When Was Wales?*, Harmondsworth: Penguin.

Wilson, F.P. (1959) 'Sir Walter Wilson Greg 1875–1959', *Proceedings of the British Academy*, vol. xlv.

Wilson, John Dover (1959) contribution to a number of obituary notices of Greg in *The Library*, 5th series, vol. xiv, No. 3, September 1959.

Wilson, John Dover (1944) (ed.) *Life in Shakespeare's England*, (Cambridge 1911), Harmondsworth: Penguin.

Wimsatt, W.K. (1969) (ed.) *Dr. Johnson on Shakespeare*, Harmondsworth: Penguin.

Wind, Edgar (1967) *Pagan Mysteries in the Renaissance*, revised edn, Harmondsworth: Penguin.

Woolf, C. and Wilson, J. Moorcroft (1982) (eds.) *Authors Take Sides on the Falklands*, London: Cecil Woolf.

Index